50 Practical and Decorative
KNOTS
You Should Know

50 Practical and Decorative
KNOTS
You Should Know

Percy W. Blandford

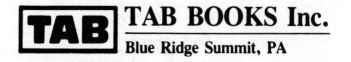

TAB BOOKS Inc.

Blue Ridge Summit, PA

FIRST EDITION
FIRST PRINTING

Library of Congress Cataloging in Publication Data

Blandford, Percy W.
50 practical and decorative knots you should know / by Percy W.
Blandford
p.   cm.
Includes index.
ISBN 0-8306-9304-1 (pbk.)
1. Knots and splices. I. Title. II. Title: Fifty practical and
decorative knots you should know.
VM533.B53   1988   88-3530
                                                                CIP

Questions regarding the content of this book
should be addressed to:

Reader Inquiry Branch
TAB BOOKS Inc.
Blue Ridge Summit, PA 17294-0214

Contents

Introduction

Ropes have been made from the earliest days of man, and knots must have been devised to use with them by primitive rope users. Throughout the centuries, the range of knots has increased according to the ingenuity of users and their needs. The numbers of knots and their names have become infinite, with much duplication as users have found similar solutions in widely separated locations.

Although ropework and knots have been necessary in a great many occupations, it was in the days of large sailing ships that they probably had the greatest impact. With their miles of rigging and the multiplicity of needs, enormous numbers of knots were needed and devised to keep these ships afloat. Those days have passed, but some traditionalists still cling to knots associated with square-rigged sailing ships, although many are now obsolete. A newcomer to knotting reading a book, not necessarily old, with a bias toward this nautical ropework might find himself learning knots no longer needed.

Seamen's knots have tended to overshadow those knots with shore applications. Of course, anyone who goes to sea today should know some knots, but it is better to consider knotting as a whole, with applications to suit circumstances which are often the same ashore and afloat.

The important consideration is finding the correct knot for a particular use, and this book is laid out to help you toward that end. There are variations, and some knots are known by more than one name, but the application to suit a need is more important than settling on a name.

This is basically a practical book intended to help any user of cordage, whether string or large hawsers, to find a suitable knot for his needs. The choice is reduced to essentials, and alternatives considered of lesser value are omitted.

This is not a book for the knotting enthusiast, although it might help him simplify his thinking. Many find an interest in knotting for its own sake, and some are joined together in the *International Guild of Knot Tyers*. If this book whets your appetite for knotting and you wish to go further, there are many larager books to help, up to the *Ashley Book of Knots* (Doubleday, Doran), with over 3,000 knots.

Chapter 1

Ropes and Cords

Cords of all sizes have been made throughout history from a large variety of natural fibers. Some of these are still used, but now many synthetic (man-made) fibers and filaments are used instead of the traditional fibers. Most of the man-made fibers are stronger and more durable than natural fibers. They will not rot and most will not absorb water. They may, however, be affected by excesses of heat or sunlight. Synthetic ropes are made of continuous filaments, so they are usually smooth. Natural fibers are short, so the rope surface is rough and hairy from the many ends protruding. This means that if what you are handling is smooth, it is synthetic, but if it is rough, it could be natural fiber or synthetic fiber made to look and feel like natural.

If a flame is applied to the end of a piece of natural fiber rope, it will char or burn. If it is synthetic material, it will melt. Natural fiber ropes have only a slight stretch. Nearly all synthetic ropes are without appreciable stretch, but nylon is very elastic and should only be used where this characteristic is an advantage. Elsewhere, it could never be pulled tight.

Ropes have been formed in many ways, but today most are three-strand or braided. In a *three-stranded rope,* the fibers are twisted into yarns, which are then twisted into strands. At each stage, the twists are reversed, so any tendency of one stage to untwist tightens the next stage. In *braided construction,* the yarns are woven over and under in opposite directions, to give a smooth cylindrical form.

Most three-stranded rope is *right-handed*. As you look along the rope, the strands twist away from you to the right. Small cords and string are specified in several ways, often by weight. In measurable sizes, it is usual to quote the diameter in fractions of an inch or millimeters. It has been the practice to quote the circumferences of large ropes used on ships. In this case, you have to divide by three to get the approximate diameter. Similarly, you may find lengths quoted in *fathoms* (six feet), but such traditional dimensions have given way to diameter and lengths in feet or meters.

Synthetic material is very much stronger, so thinner lines can be used than would be needed for natural materials, but you may have to consider practicalities, such as handling. If it is a rope you have to haul, ⅜-inch diameter is the thinnest on which to get a comfortable grip, although a cord only half that diameter might be strong enough for the purpose.

There are many knots that had traditional uses with natural fiber ropes. With smooth slippery synthetic ropes, some of these knots are unsafe because there are not enough turns to grip securely. The knots to use with modern materials are either developments of these knots with extra turns or entirely new knots.

Traditionists say a *knot* is made in one rope, a *bend* is used to join ropes, and a *hitch* attaches a rope to a post or ring. Unfortunately, there are so many contradictions that you cannot rigidly apply these terms. It is safe to use the word *knot* as the general term to embrace all of them (Fig. 1-1).

Most rope will unlay itself if a cut end is left unprotected, and most synthetics cannot be laid up again successfully, so you have to cut again and waste some rope. To hold the rope strands temporarily, you can bind with adhesive tape and cut through the tape (Fig. 1-2A). Heat will melt fiber ends together and prevent them unlaying. There are cutting devices available in which a heated knife cuts and seals both parts in one action. You can seal a cut end by heating it in the flame of a match or cigarette lighter until the fibers are melting, then wet your finger and thumb and roll the end tightly.

For small lines, sealing in this way should be adequate, but for larger cords and ropes, and for all natural fiber lines larger than string, the end should be *whipped*. This is in addition to any heat sealing of synthetics.

A *whipping* is a very tight binding with thin line. Within reason, the thinner the line in relation to the rope, the stronger

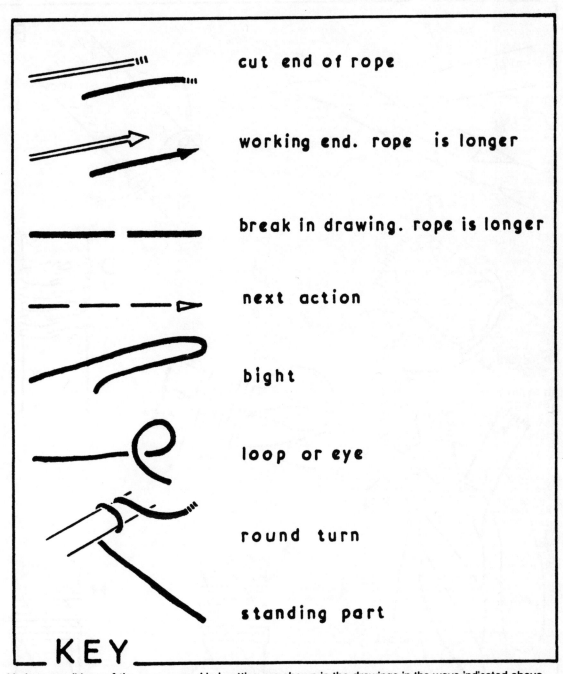

cut end of rope

working end. rope is longer

break in drawing. rope is longer

next action

bight

loop or eye

round turn

standing part

KEY

Various conditions of the rope or cord in knotting are shown in the drawings in the ways indicated above.

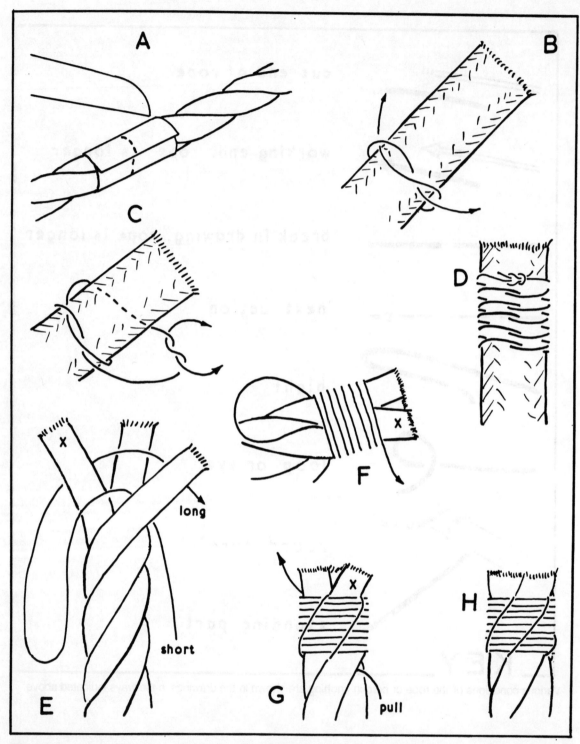

Fig. 1-1. Rope being cut may be prevented from unlaying by binding with adhesive tape (A). A *West Country whipping* is knotted (B,C,D). A *sailmaker's whipping* goes through and around the rope (E–H).

will be the whipping. It could be natural or synthetic fiber. Sewing thread is suitable for most commonly used ropes. Rubbing the line with wax helps to make the whipping stay in place, particularly when holding turns as they are made—a whipping is of no use if it is allowed to slip as it is made and become loose.

Of the large numbers of whippings that have been devised, two are suggested for all circumstances. You might even settle for the first only. This is called a *West Country whipping.* The other is a *sailmaker's whipping.*

To make a *West Country whipping,* put the middle of a line behind the rope a short distance from its end. Bring the ends to the front and tie an *overhand knot* (Fig. 1-2B) tightly. Go to the back and do the same (Fig. 1-2C). Continue doing this at back and front alternately, with the turns close together, until you have traveled a distance no more than the diameter of the rope, or ½-inch if it is a very thick rope. Finish by making the last overhand knot into a *reef knot* (Fig. 1-2D).

The West Country whipping can be used on rope of any construction, but the sailmaker's whipping is only suitable for three-strand rope. Used thus, it is then very secure, because it goes through as well as around the rope. It is possible to make it with the help of a needle, but with this method you only use your fingers.

Open the end of the rope for a short distance. Lay in a loop of whipping line, enclosing one strand and with a long and a short end projecting from the opposite space (Fig. 1-2E). Hold the parts of the whipping line down the rope, out of the way, and lay up the strands again. Using the long end, put on sufficient tight turns (Fig. 1-2F). Lift the loop over the end of the strand it is already around and pull the short end to tighten it (Fig. 1-2G). This puts snaking turns outside the turns round the rope, following the spaces between strands. Take the short end over the remaining space and into the center of the end of the rope to meet the long end. Tie them together tightly in the middle of the rope and cut off surplus line, to complete the whipping (Fig. 1-2H).

If it is synthetic rope, seal the end with heat. With any whipped rope do not trim the end too close to the whipping—upwards of ¼ inch should project.

Chapter 2

Knots in a Single Line

If you want to prevent a rope pulling through your hand, a hole, or back through anything it has passed through, you need to tie a knot in it to enlarge the rope. Such knots are collectively called *stopper knots,* but they have other uses besides stopping. They may be tied in a rope to assist climbing, they might be tied in a cord to mark distances when measuring, or they could mark a position on a rope for locating in the dark.

The obvious choice is a *simple twist* (Fig. 2-1A), which has many names — *thumb* and *overhand* are common ones. In this book, we call it *overhand.* For many purposes, it is all you need.

Overhand knots are sometimes made in the end of a rope to prevent it unlaying. That ought to be regarded as only a temporary expedient. The rope end should be sealed and/or whipped. A knot may be the only way of dealing with thread or thin string, but if it is synthetic, sealing is preferable.

If the lump formed by pulling an overhand knot tight is not as large as you need, the next choice is a *figure-eight knot.* Start as if you are making an overhand knot, but go around the other side (Fig. 2-1B) and pass through from there (Fig. 2-1C). When pulled tight, the result is a thicker stopper.

Both knots can be made slightly thicker and made easier to release if you tuck a *bight,* or *loop,* instead of an end (Fig. 2-1D and E). The figure-eight knot is used as the base for some knots described later, so it helps to be familiar with forming it, even if you rarely need it as a stopper.

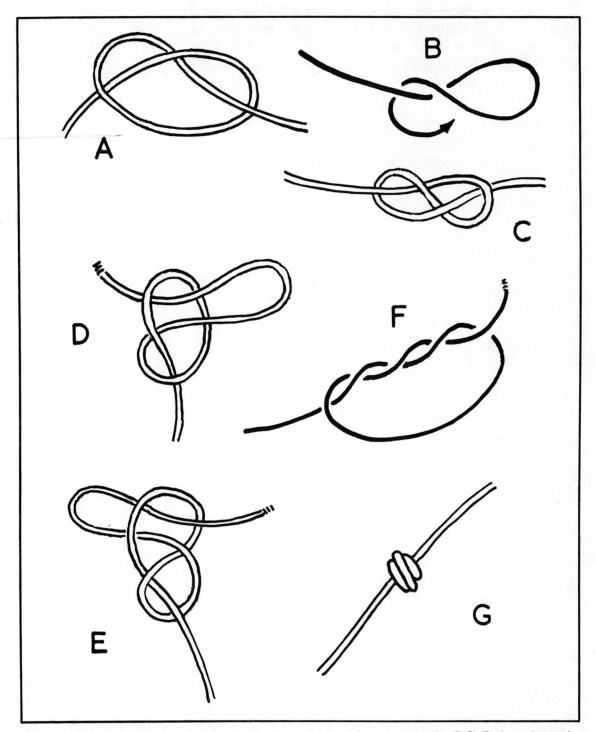

Fig. 2-1. An *overhand knot* is a simple twist (A). *Figure-eight knot* has an extra twist (B,C). Both can be made quick-release by tucking a *bight* (D,E). Extra turns of a *blood knot* make a bigger stopper (F,G).

One way of making an even bigger stopper is to use a *blood knot*, which is a simple development of an overhand knot. Make an overhand knot, then put in one or two more turns (Fig. 2-1F) before pulling tight. The large part of the loop will close into turns round the twisting you have done (Fig. 2-1G).

Chapter 3

Joining Knots

The most frequent knotting need is to join the end of one cord to the end of another. For this purpose, most people select a *reef knot,* although that is not always the result they get, and for many purposes it is not the right knot. Modern thought on end-to-end knots has changed with the advent of synethetics.

A *reef knot,* or *square knot,* is made by twisting the two ends together, then twisting them again the other way (Fig. 3-1A). If you have made the knot correctly, the two ends will project from the knot alongside their own standing parts (Fig. 3-1B). What many people do, however, is make the two twists the same way, to result in a *granny knot* (Fig. 3-1C). When pulled tight, the ends project across the knot (Fig. 3-1D). A granny knot will slip and should never be used by anyone who claims to know something of knotting.

The reef knot has limited uses. It is only satisfactory when it is bearing against something. It is not the joining knot to use if it will not be resting against a support. The name comes from the knot's use in the old method of reefing a sail, when the reef points were joined with this knot under the boom or under a tight roll of canvas. It is the usual knot for bandaging, when it will bear against a limb or other part of the body. It is satisfactory where the joined cords will be wrapped around something solid. The reef knot is suitable for string, cord, and thinner ropes, but for larger ropes there are better knots.

If the second twist of a reef knot is made with one end turned

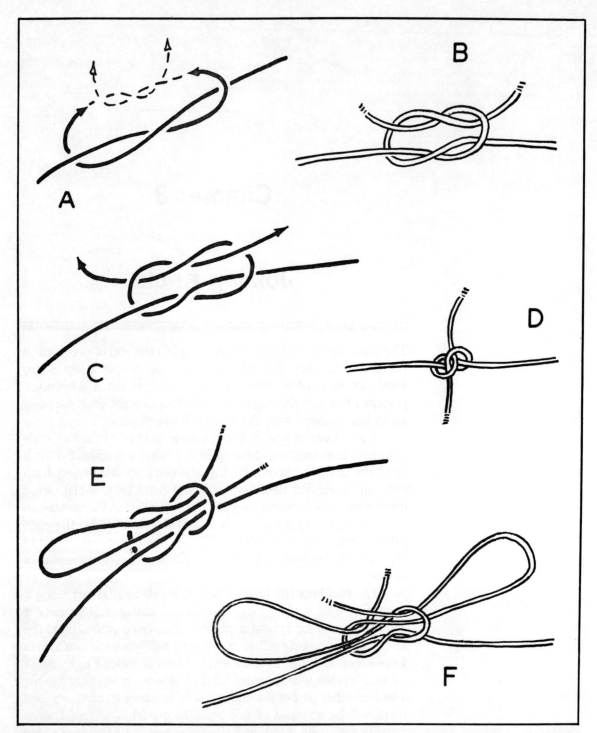

Fig. 3-1. In a *reef knot,* the ends finish alongside the standing parts (A,B). In an unsafe *granny knot,* they finish across (C,D). The reef can be finished as a *single* or *double bow* (E,F).

back in a bight, you have a *single reef bow* or a *slip reef* (Fig. 3-1E), which can be released by pulling the end from the bight. If you make both parts of the second twist with bights, you have made a *double reef bow* (Fig. 3-1F). That should be the bow used when shoe laces are tied. The loops of the bow are then across your foot. If they are in an up-and-down direction, you have made a *granny bow,* which may not matter much, except for your prestige as a knot tier.

The traditional joining knot was known as the *common bend* or the *sheet bend,* from its oldtime use in joining the sheet (controlling rope) to a sail. This is still a good joining knot for many purposes, but with smooth synthetics it may not be good enough. To make the knot, turn one end back on itself to form a bight. Bring the other end up through it (Fig. 3-2A), around the back (Fig. 3-2B), then across the front of the bight under its own part (Fig. 3-2C). Be careful to keep the cords in this formation as you pull the knot tight. It is usual to tuck the parts so both ends finish on the same side of the knot.

If the ropes are of different thicknesses, make the bight in the thicker one (Fig. 3-2D). If there is very much difference in thickness, take the thinner one around a second time to make a *double sheet bend* (Fig. 3-2E and F). This is essential if there is much difference in the rope diameters and almost always essential with slippery synthetics, even if they are the same diameter.

Both forms of the knot may be made quick-release by tucking the working end with a bight (Fig. 3-2G).

Fishermen have developed many knots for their own use, particularly on fine slippery line. One that has gained in importance has been what the general user of knots has called a *fisherman's knot,* which now has more uses with rather bigger lines than was originally intended, due to its holding power on synthetic fiber ropes.

In the basic fisherman's knot, one end is brought through an overhand knot in the end of the other line (Fig. 3-3A), then taken further along to make its own overhand knot (Fig. 3-3B). As you pull tight, the two overhand knots bed against each other (Fig. 3-3C). Make sure the overhand knots are made so the projecting ends come alongside the line. If a knot is twisted the other way, the two parts will not bed neatly together.

A *double fisherman's knot* has each overhand knot taken round a second time (Fig. 3-3D and E). This increases bulk, but the extra turns increase grip. Mountaineers and rock climbers, whose lives may depend on knots in the synthetic rope they use,

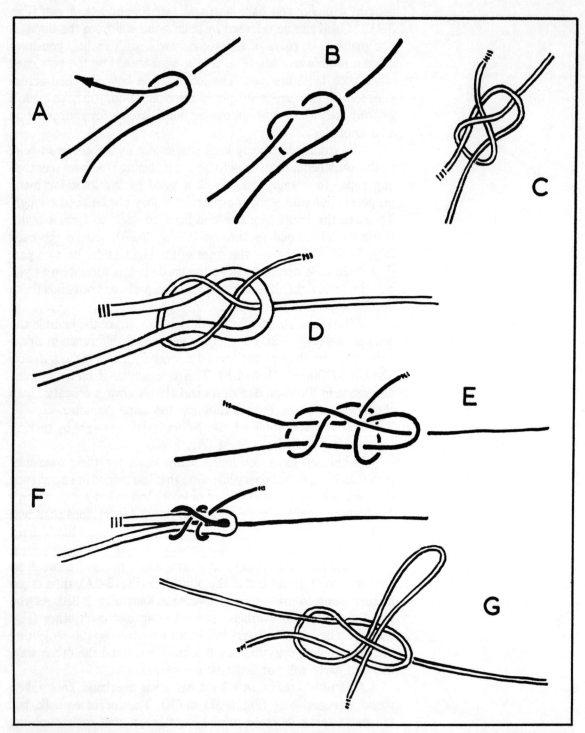

Fig. 3-2. In a *sheet bend,* one end is worked around a bight of the other (A–D). *Double sheet bend* has an extra turn (E,F). Either form may be made quick-release with a bight (G).

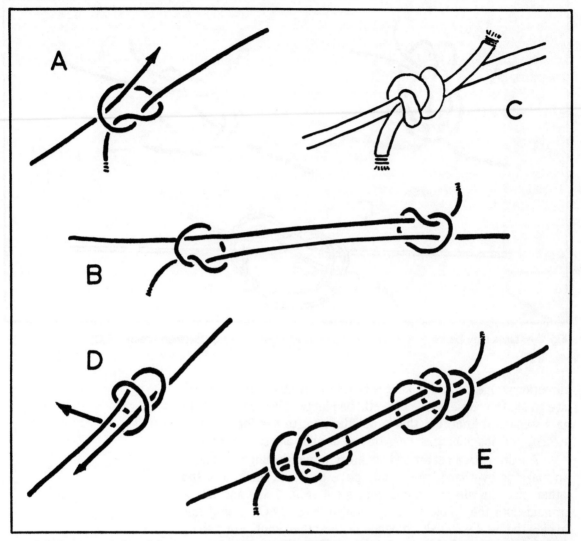

Fig. 3-3. *Fisherman's knot* links two overhand knots (A,B,C). Extra strength comes from doubling them (D,E).

have experimented with knots, and modern mountaineering research has discarded the reef knot and sheet bend, and the joining knot recommended is the double fisherman's knot. Other rope users may wish to follow their lead. A fisherman using the knot on thin line may call this a *barrel knot* or another *blood knot*.

Any knot is weaker than the line from which it is made. The greatest loss of strength is when there are sharp bends in the parts of a knot. For this reason it is unwise to join ropes by holding the ends together and tying an overhand knot with them (Fig. 3-4A). Under load the two parts of this *overhand bend* pulling in opposite

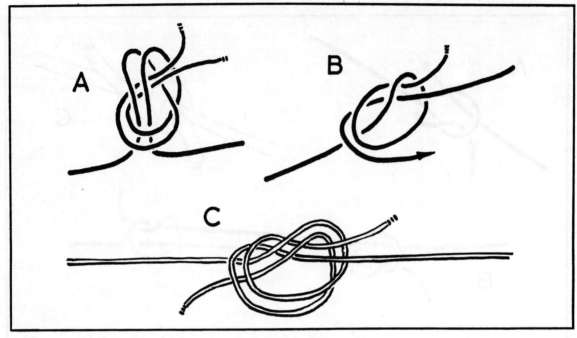

Fig. 3-4. Lines may be joined with an *overhand bend* together (A) or followed around (B,C).

directions come out of the knot with relatively sharp bends, which are weak. Of course, there may still be plenty of reserve strength in a weakened knot, but this is not the knot to use for anything except perhaps joining sewing thread or thin pieces of string.

An alternative neater and stronger way of joining thin line is to make an overhand knot in one piece and take the end of the other piece in where the end comes out (Fig. 3-4B) and follow around until the whole knot is doubled (Fig. 3-4C). Doing this avoids the weakening sharp bends of the other knot. For fishing line, this may be called a *ring knot.* Izaac Walton, the father figure of fishing, calls it a *water knot.*

At the other extreme is the need to join very large, and often stiff, ropes. It is impossible or very difficult to use any of the knots appropriate to lighter and more flexible lines. If you are faced with the problem of joining large ropes, or even smaller ropes which are very stiff, the knot to use is the *carrick bend.* You may find other uses for it as the base for some decorative ropework.

Older seamanship books give several versions of the carrick bend, but the strongest uses an over and under weaving technique in putting it together. Bend one end back under itself to make a large loop (Fig. 3-5A). Lay the other end under it (Fig. 3-5B), then

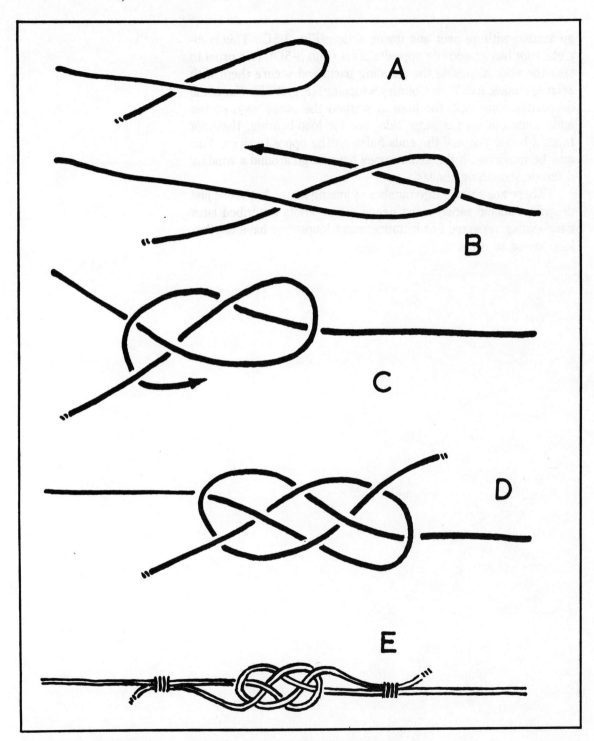

Fig. 3-5. In a *carrick bend,* the lines are joined in an over and under weave.

go around with an over and under action (Fig. 3-5C). This complete knot has its ends on opposite sides (Fig. 3-5D). It is usual to take the ends alongside the standing parts and secure them with *seizings* (made like West Country whipping) (Fig. 3-5E). For some decorative ropework, the knot is worked the other way, so the ends come out on the same side, but for load-bearing, the knot takes a better shape if the ends finish on the opposite sides. This may be important if the joined ropes have to go around a winding drum or something similar.

There are a very large number of joining knots, but those just described should satisfy most needs. Some knots described later have joining versions. For instance, most loops may have another loop joined to them.

Chapter 4

A Loop in the End of a Line

The simplest way to put a loop in the end of a line is to turn back a bight and tie an overhand knot, making an *overhand-knot-on-a-bight* (Fig. 4-1A). This has a few uses, but in most circumstances it would be unwise to rely on this knot. It will make a loop in the end of a piece of thread or fine string and may take any load expected to be put on it. In smooth synthetic fishing line or other fine cord, it will probably slip. There are superior knots for making loops in larger cords and ropes.

A better knot, in any case, is a *figure-eight-on-a-bight*. Use a bight in the end of a line and make a figure eight in it (Fig. 4-1B). This has possibilities for any line, from thread up to climbing ropes. Climbers limit its use and add an overhand knot with the end around the standing part (Fig. 4-1C).

There are occasions in climbing and in other circumstances, when you need to tie the loop around your body or something else and complete it to the size you need. It is possible to do this with the figure-eight-on-a-bight. Make an open figure-eight knot, with enough end hanging to make the loop and complete the knot (Fig. 4-1D). Take the end around yourself or the object, then lead it in reverse into the knot (Fig. 4-1E) and follow around until it is doubled (Fig. 4-1F), then pull tight. Add the overhand knot, if it is required.

This version of the figure-eight knot is easy to form, but you cannot easily adjust its size, except in the manner just described. If it is subject to much loading, it may be difficult to untie. If you have

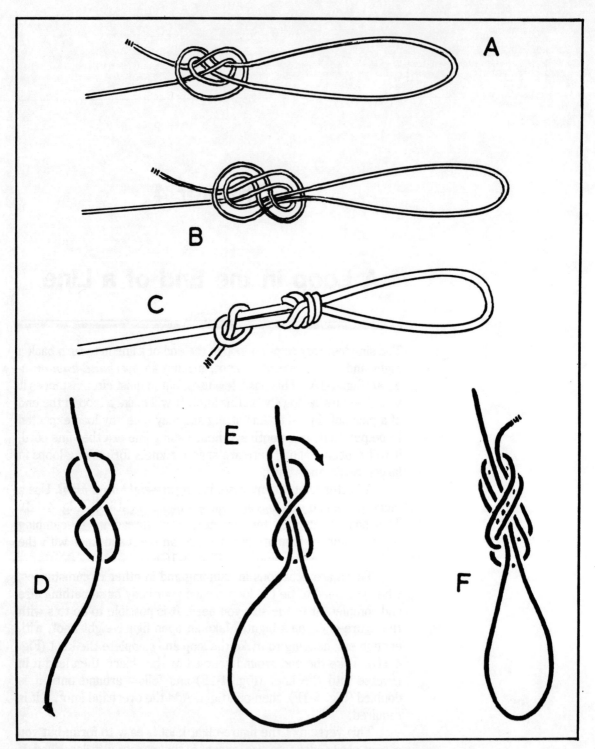

Fig. 4-1. An *end loop* may be formed with an overhand or *figure-eight-on-a-bight*.

to choose between this and an overhand-knot-on-a-bight, however, always choose the figure-eight-on-a-bight. For most purposes, one of the following loop knots is preferable.

The knot for making a loop in the end of a line, which is often accepted as the example of all a knot should be, is the *bowline* (Fig. 4-2A). A bowline can be used to make a loop of any size. The knot does not normally slip, it keeps its shape and is easy to undo after being loaded.

The name comes from the use of the knot on the bow line of a sailing ship, There are several versions of the bowline, but the basic type is all that will be required for most purposes. It is easiest to learn with cord or rope of moderate size, but it can be applied to almost any line.

There are some special ways of forming a bowline, but for the first attempt, so as to understand the form the knot must take, have the cord on a flat surface. Allow enough length for the required loop and twist a small eye, with the standing part under the loop part (Fig. 4-2B). Hold the eye in shape and pass the end up through it (Fig. 4-2C). Go round the standing part and down through the eye between the sides of the loop (Fig. 4-2D). Keep the knot in this form as you pull it tight. If you pull the standing part one way and the sides of the loop and the end the opposite way, the knot should keep its shape. If you examine the knot, you will see that the arrangement of crossings is the same as a sheet bend. See that it keeps this shape. Once tightened it will not go out of shape, but incorrect tightening could distort it into a *slip knot*.

The method of forming the bowline just described is perfectly acceptable, but there is a quick method worth knowing, if the bowline is to be around your own waist or some other solid object. Treat this as a second method, not an only method, because you would look silly if you had to tie the bowline round your own waist first before removing it to use for another purpose.

Put the end over the standing part (Fig. 4-2E). With some slack in the standing part, turn the end under towards the loop (Fig. 4-2F) and upwards, so it is pulled straight (Fig. 4-2G). This can be done with one hand, gripping the crossing together and turning over with one action. That leaves only the end to pass round and down into the eye you have formed.

A basically similar method, more suitable when the loop does not have to be around anything solid, is to make an overhand knot (Fig. 4-2H) and pull the end straight (Fig. 4-2J), so it is ready to complete a bowline. Climbers join the hanging end to the side of the loop with an overhand knot (Fig. 4-2K).

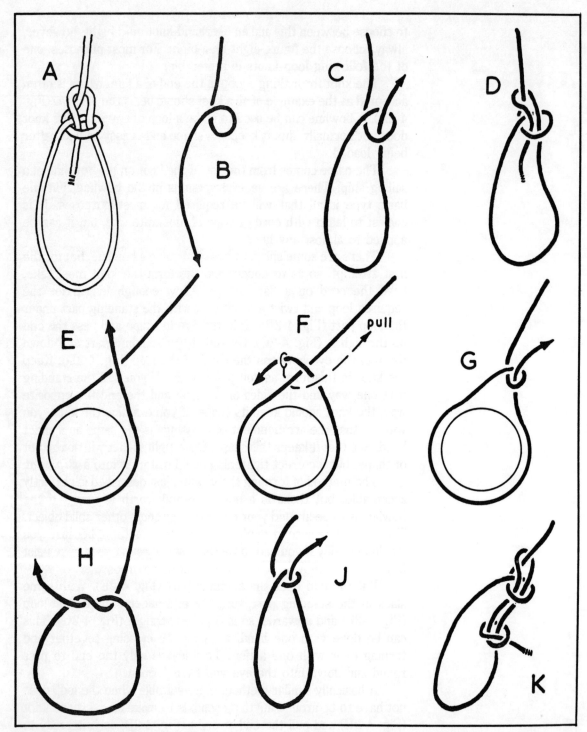

Fig. 4-2. *Bowline* (A) may be formed by following around (B,C,D), by pulling around an object (E,F,G) or by converting an overhand knot (H,J,K).

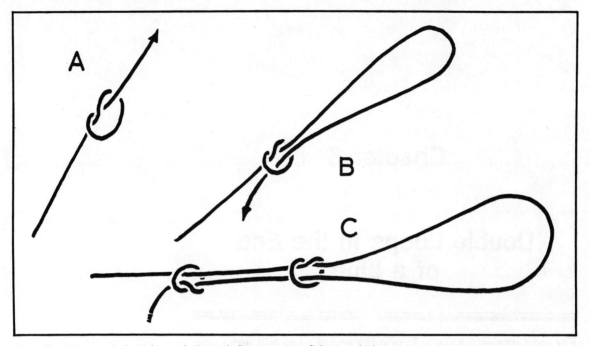

Fig 4-3. *Fisherman's loop* is made in a similar way to a fisherman's knot.

For fine line, there is a *fisherman's loop*, based on the fisherman's knot. Make an overhand knot, far enough back to allow enough line to make the loop (Fig. 4-3A). Pass the end back through it (Fig. 4-3B), then make an overhand knot with the end around the other piece (Fig. 4-3C). As with the fisherman's knot, make the overhand knots so the parts are alongside each other, and the two overhand knots bed together when drawn tight. For extra security with very slippery lines, the two overhand knots can be doubled, as described for the double fisherman's knot (Fig. 3-3D and E).

The fisherman's loop has several other names in old manuals. There is a method of forming it without using the ends. It is then called a *middleman's knot* (Fig. 6-1D). Although that method could be used for a loop at an end, it is easier to get the loop the size you want by the method just described.

A loop formed with a knot may be regarded as temporary. It should be possible to undo the knot when the loop is no longer needed. As with any knot, a loop knot is weaker than the rope from which it is formed, but the margin of safety will usually be much more than adequate. The only thing stronger than a loop knot is an *eye splice* (Fig. 16-1). This is a permanent loop, and its strength is greater in relation to that of the rope than any knot.

Chapter 5

Double Loops in the End
of a Line

For most purposes a single loop in the end of a line will serve your needs. For lifting some loads, however, it may be better to have a double loop. If you want to lift or lower a person, a double loop can be arranged under his arms and under his knees, so he is held in a sitting position.

The double loop knot for nearly all purposes is the *bowline-on-a-bight*. It has the bowline formation, but is finished in a special way. Turn back a long bight, slightly more than enough to form the required double loop. At a suitable position, form a small eye, with the standing parts behind (Fig. 5-1A), then pass the end of the bight up through it (Fig. 5-1B). Up to this stage the formation is the same as a single bowline, but instead of passing the end of the bight around the standing parts, hold the eye in shape and pull through enough of the end of the bight to pass back over the loops (Fig. 5-1C), until it closes around the standing parts, to complete the knot (Fig. 5-1D). Hold the eye in shape as you tighten. At this stage, you can pull through the line to vary the relative sizes of the loops, if you want one bigger than the other.

The load may be taken by both standing parts, but if there is just one long standing part for lifting, and the short part is free alongside it, there should be little risk of slipping. For added security, an overhand knot may be made with it around the long part (Fig. 5-1E), close to the bowline formation.

The bowline-on-a-bight is suitable for anything from moderate-size cord up to large ropes, but it is not so successful with

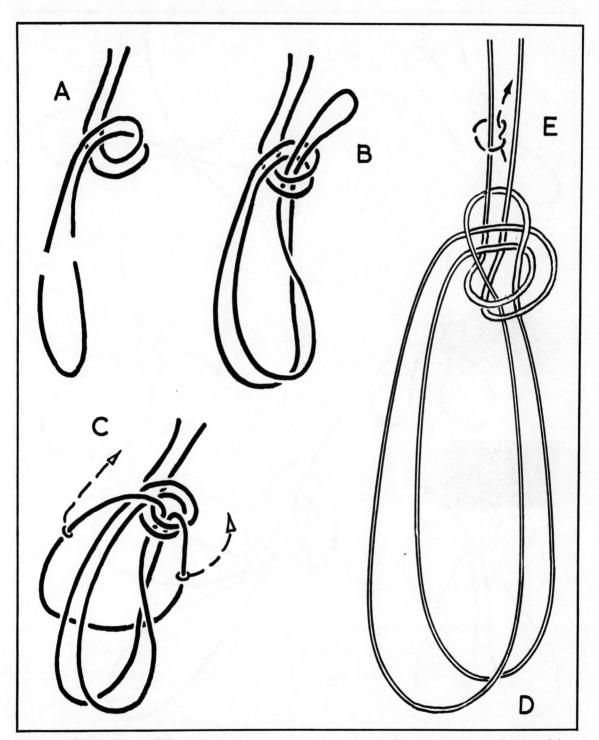

Fig. 5-1. *Bowline-on-a-bight* starts like single bowline (A,B), but the end of the bight goes over the rest of the knot (C) to complete it (D,E).

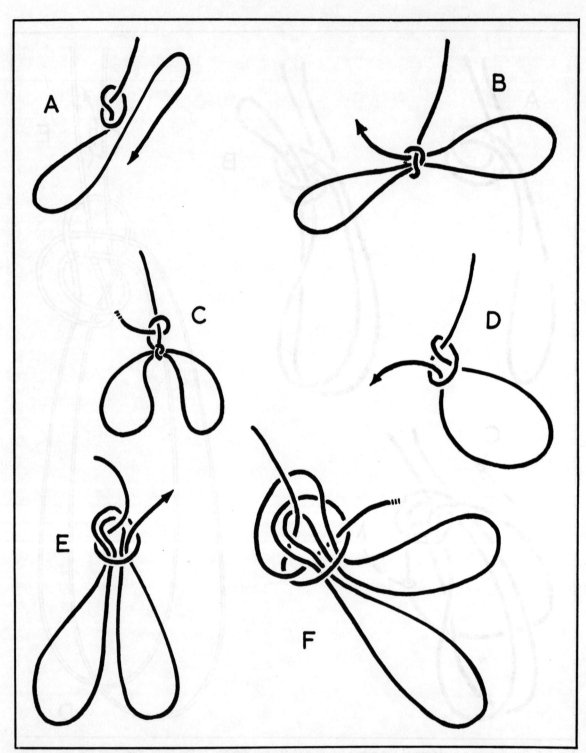

Fig. 5-2. *Forked loop knot* is suitable for fine line and can be made in the two ways shown.

fishing line, thin string, or thread. A simple double loop in the end of this fine line is a *forked loop knot.* Make a loose overhand knot far enough back from the end to allow for the two loops (Fig. 5-2A). Pass a bight of the end back through the knot (Fig. 5-2B) and adjust the resulting two loops to the sizes you want them. Pull the knot tight and take the end round the standing part. Either just tuck it under itself (Fig. 5-2C) or make an overhand knot with it.

The forked loop knot finishes with the loops on opposite sides. Another version may be called a *close-forked loop knot* and has the two loops touching and in line with the standing part.

Make an overhand knot with the working end as a bight only partly pulled through (Fig. 5-2D). Take the end back around the standing part, so you can put another bight through the overhand knot (Fig. 5-2E). Adjust these two loops to the sizes you want. Take the end behind the standing part and across the turn of the overhand knot behind the upper parts of the loop (Fig. 5-2F). This will lock the knot as you pull it tight.

Like most other fine line knots, the two forked loop knots are almost impossible to undo when they have been tightened under load. The bowline-on-a-bight should usually be easy to cast off.

Chapter 6

A Loop Away from the Ends

Sometimes you need a loop in the body of a rope or cord nowhere near the ends. On a climbing rope already attached to other climbers or a belay at the ends, you may have to loop around the waist of another person. You may want to make a loop to put your shoulder in to help haul a load. You may want to put in a small loop to mark a distance along a rope. It would be tedious to form a loop that involves drawing an end through if the total length of line is considerable.

The figure-eight-on-a-bight is one possibility. This has already been described for use at the end of a rope (Fig. 4-1). You could gather up a bight anywhere along a rope and make this knot. It is also possible to use a bowline-on-a-bight (Fig. 5-1), as this is formed without having to tuck an end.

The fisherman's knot loop, as described for the end of fine line (Fig. 4-3) can be made in another way without having to pass an end through at any stage. It is not so easy to regulate the size of the resulting loop, however. Turn back a bight on itself (Fig. 6-1A). Cross the two loops you have formed (Fig. 6-1B). Grasp the middle of the bight and pull it up through the crossing (Fig. 6-1C). This forms the two parts into the overhand knots of a fisherman's knot, but you may have to experiment with shaking or pulling the turns into position in your early attempts. With cord or small rope, it is easier to see what is happening than with thin line. The result is a fisherman's loop or *middleman's knot* (Fig. 6-1D). This is not a climber's knot for around a waist, because a pull in one direction

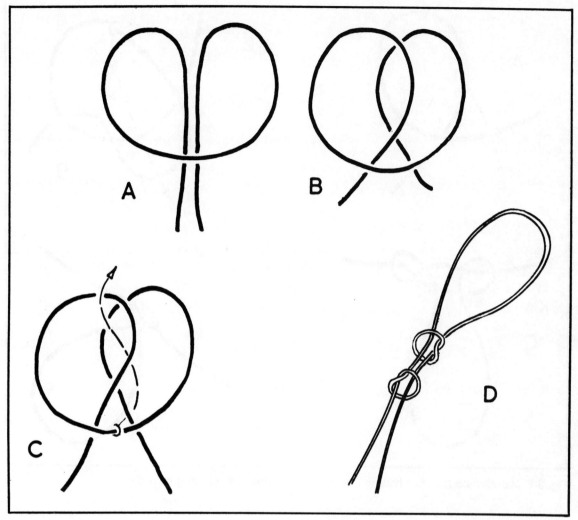

Fig. 6-1. *Middleman's knot* is similar to a fisherman's loop, but is made without using the ends of the line.

will make it slip and reduce the size of the loop. For fishing and many other purposes, however, this would not be a hazard. The knot can also be treated as a puzzle, or a demonstration of your skill in front of the uninitiated!

The *man-harness knot* is the traditional way of putting a loop in a rope to help in dragging a load. Its other name of *artillery loop* comes from its use in the ropes attached to gun carriages. It is a safe knot, providing it is kept in shape as it is tightened. If allowed to pull out of shape at this stage, it could slip so the loop gets smaller.

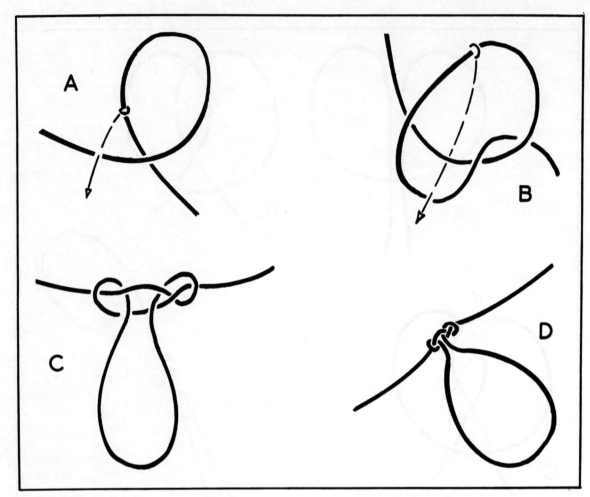

Fig. 6-2. *Man-harness knot* is a hauling loop to put in a rope without using its ends.

Twist the rope into a loop slightly bigger than will finally be needed (Fig. 6-2A). Lift the side of the loop over the part it is already under (Fig. 6-2B). Take the other side through the space you have formed (Fig. 6-2C). Pull through all the slack loop, while keeping the twists of the knot in shape (Fig. 6-2D). Finally, tighten on the standing parts.

Chapter 7

A Rope to a Pole

There are many occasions when most of us want to tie a rope to a pole, ring, or something else solid. The special knots needed are more correctly called *hitches*. It is possible to use some of the knots already described, but there are a few others worth learning.

If what you want to attach to has an open end, such as a post driven into the ground, a bollard on a dock side, or a hook, you can have your rope already prepared with a bowline (Fig. 4-2) in its end. This is helpful if you have to secure the rope quickly, as when in a boat coming up to a dock in a fast flowing stream. You can put the prepared rope over, without having to spend time knotting. Even better is an eye splice (Fig. 16-1).

If the loop is long, you can strengthen the grip by putting on a second turn (Fig. 7-1A). Any time a rope completely encircles something solid in this way it is called a *round turn*. It occurs in some other knots, and the friction it causes adds considerably to the strength of the fastening.

If it is a more permanent fastening, such as a rope to the ring in the bow of an open boat, pass the end of the bowline loop through the ring and the end of the rope through it (Fig. 7-1B). You can do the same on a post, but if its end is available, bend back the loop first and put the resulting two rings over it (Fig. 7-1C). This is one way of tethering an animal to limit its grazing.

You should learn to tie a *clove hitch*. Besides its use alone, it occurs in several other knots, ties, and lashings, and it helps to be able to make it correctly each time. To make a clove hitch round a

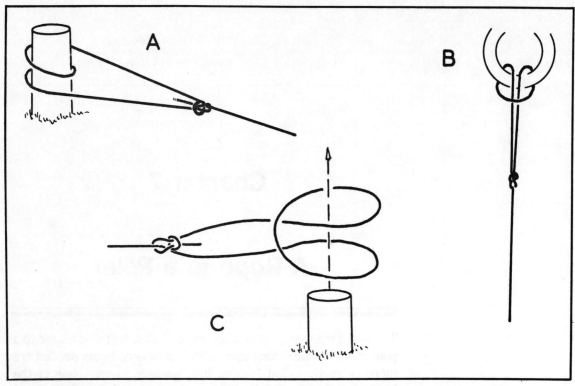

Fig. 7-1. A long *bowline loop* may take a round turn on a post (A), loop through a ring (B), or be half hitched on a post (C).

pole or through a ring, use only one end. Put the end over the pole and go around over the standing part (Fig. 7-2A). Continue around the same way and under itself (Fig. 7-2B). For a first time it helps to keep the two turns wide apart so you see the action, but in the finished hitch they should be close together (Fig. 7-2C). Each turn is a *half hitch* and in some books this is described as a jamming form of *two-half hitches*.

If it is an open-ended post or the point of a hook, you can make the clove hitch first and slip it over. Turn a loop in the rope and then a similar one above it (Fig. 7-2D) and put it over the end.

A common error with both ways of making a clove hitch is to change direction for the second turn. If you do this, the result is a hitch called a *cow hitch* or *lark's head* (Fig. 7-2E), which has a few uses, particularly when you want both ends to come out alongside each other, such as in the string of a luggage label (Fig. 7-2F).

If the two parts of a clove hitch are pulled opposite ways, the result is an *Oklahoma hitch* (Fig. 7-2G), which increases the friction grip when stretching a rope fence along a series of posts.

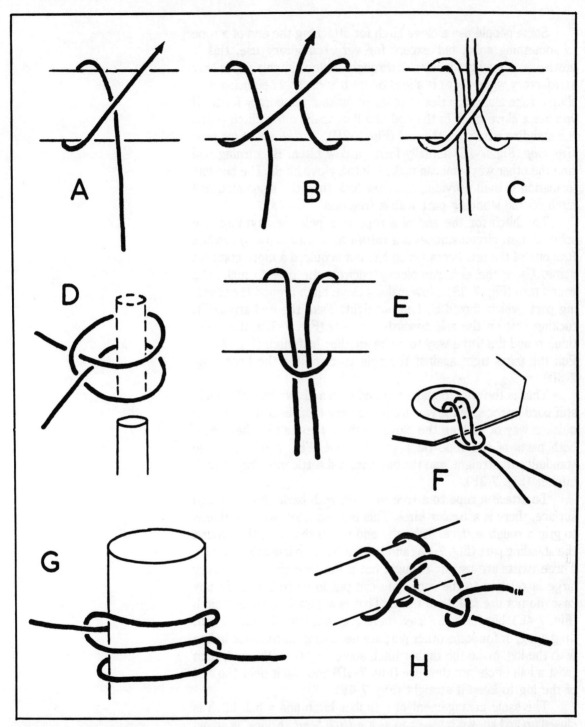

Fig. 7-2. In a *clove hitch* (A–D), two half hitches jam together. If the second hitch is the other way, it becomes a *cow hitch* (E,F). Distorting a clove hitch makes an *Oklahoma hitch* (G). A half hitch secures a clove hitch (H).

Some people use a clove hitch for attaching the end of a rope to something solid, but except for very temporary use, this is unwise, as it may gradually pull through. A clove hitch alone is only satisfactory when there is a load on both ends, as when using it to sling a rope along a series of poles to make a temporary fence. If you use a clove hitch in the end of a line, make a half hitch round the standing part with the end (Fig. 7-2H). The *double-back bowline loop* (Fig. 7-1C) actually forms a cow hitch. By turning one ring the other way, you can make it into a clove hitch. The bowline formation is then providing a better lock than the suggested half hitch on the standing part with a free end.

The hitch for the end of a rope to a pole, or anything else solid, in most circumstances is a *round turn and two half hitches*. It is one of the few knots which has not acquired a more compact name. Using the end, completely encircle the pole to make the round turn (Fig. 7-3A). Now make a clove hitch around the standing part, which should be kept straight. Take the end around it, tucking first on the side towards the pole (Fig. 7-3B), then continue round the same way to make another half hitch (Fig. 7-3C). Pull the parts tight against the pole to complete the knot (Fig. 7-3D).

That is the way to make a round turn and two half hitches in stiff cord or rope, but if you are using very flexible cord there is a quicker way of making the clove hitch or two half hitches. With both parts of the rope tie a granny knot (Fig. 7-3E). Pull the standing part straight, and the end part will settle into the two half hitches (Fig. 7-3F).

To attach a rope to a tree or a log with bark on or a rough surface, there is a *timber hitch*. This is a slip knot, which tightens to grip a rough surface. Take the end round the tree, then round the standing part (Fig. 7-4A) and twist it back on itself (Fig. 7-4B). Three twists are usually enough, but if the tree diameter is very large in relation to the rope, you can put in more twists. In any case, do not use less than three. That is a complete timber hitch (Fig. 7-4C), but for some uses there are additions. If you want to drag a log, or for some other purpose need to keep the rope in line with the log, make the timber hitch some way from the end, then twist a half hitch into the rope (Fig. 7-4D) and slip it over the end of the log to keep it straight (Fig. 7-4E).

The same arrangement of a timber hitch and a half hitch is closed up and known by seamen as a *killick bend*. 'Killick' is an old term for anchor and the bend is made round a rock (Fig. 7-4F) for use as a temporary anchor. The method may be used for anything

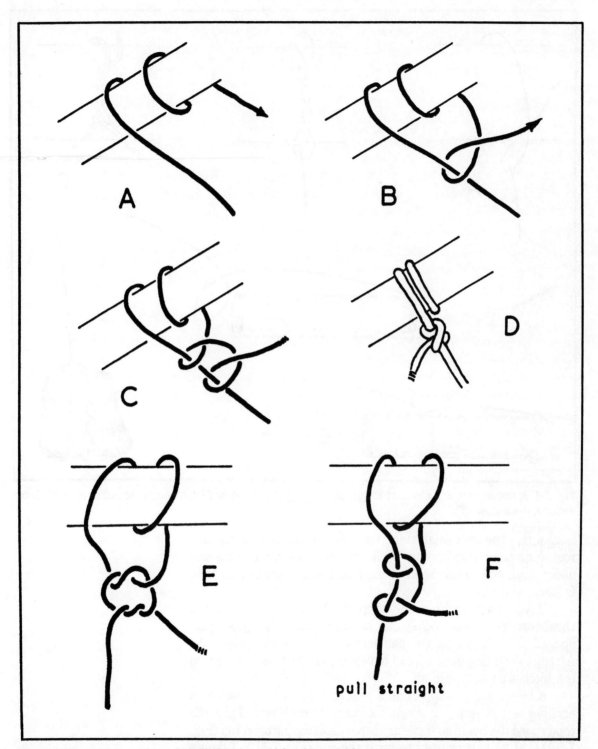

Fig. 7-3. *Round turn and two half hitches* is used for the end of a rope to a spar.

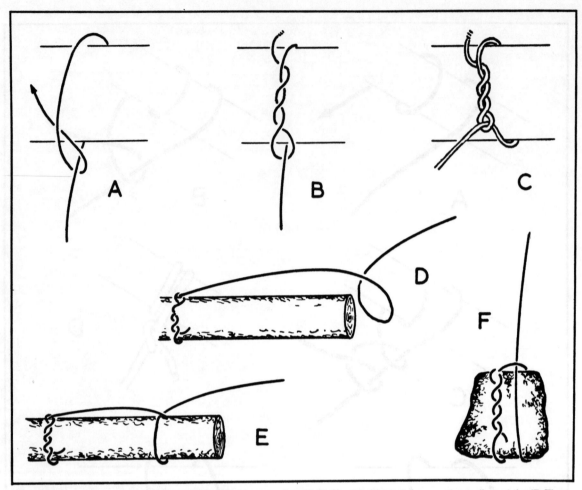

Fig. 7-4. A *timber hitch* is a slip knot to tighten on a log (A,B,C). A *half hitch* keeps the pull straight (D,E) or forms a *killick bend* (F).

from a thin line on a small stone for a fishing sinker to a massive rock for a large boat anchor. Unlike many knots, after being wet under load, the killick bend is easy to release when you have finished with it.

If you want to lower or support a pole horizontally, the Oklahoma hitch (Fig. 7-2G) can be made with its center part opened out to separate the half hitches towards the pole ends. Arrange the lifting parts spread outwards, rather than inwards, so the hitches do not close up.

A better way of supporting a pole or a board to be used as a hanging seat is to use a *scaffold hitch* near each end. Take the rope round the board so there are three crossing parts on top (Fig. 7-5A). Lift #1 part over #2 towards the end (Fig. 7-5B). Take up

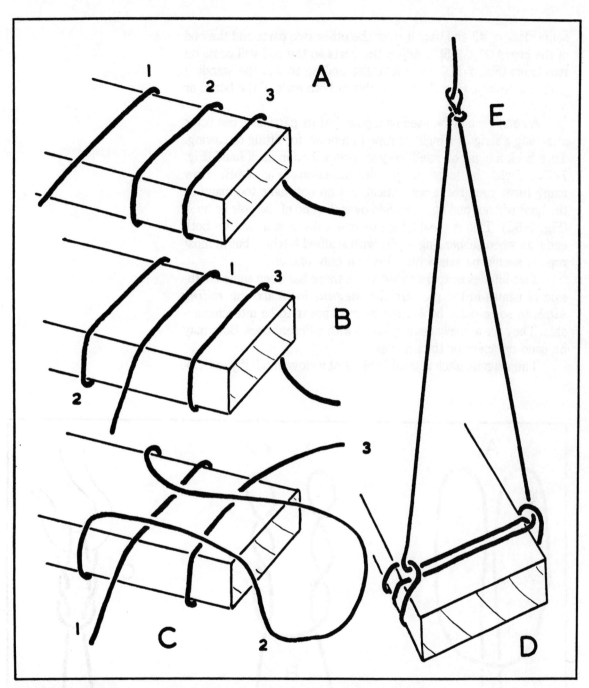

Fig. 7-5. *Scaffold hitch* supports the end of a board forming a seat or platform.

some slack of #2 and pass it over the other two parts and the end of the board (Fig. 7-5C). Adjust the parts so the pull will come on two loops (Fig. 7-5D), then take the end up to join the standing part in a bowline (Fig. 7-5E). Do this at both ends of the board or pole.

A *catspaw* may be used on a pole, but its particular use is for attaching a sling or a bight of rope to a hook, for lifting or towing. Turn back a bight on itself, so you have a loop in each hand (Fig. 7-6A). Twist the loops in opposite directions (Fig. 7-6B). How many turns you give is not critical, but do not make too many or the knot will not pull up close. Slip over the end of the pole or hook (Fig. 7-6C). This is meant for use when there is a load on both ends, as when suspending a seat with scaffold hitches, but in most rope it should be safe with a load on only one end.

Two hitches to spars about which there has been some confusion of names in the past are the *magnus hitch* and the *rolling hitch*. In some older books, the names appear to be interchangeable. They are actually distinct knots with different uses. Both may be used on spars or thicker ropes.

The magnus hitch is used in place of a clove hitch if you think

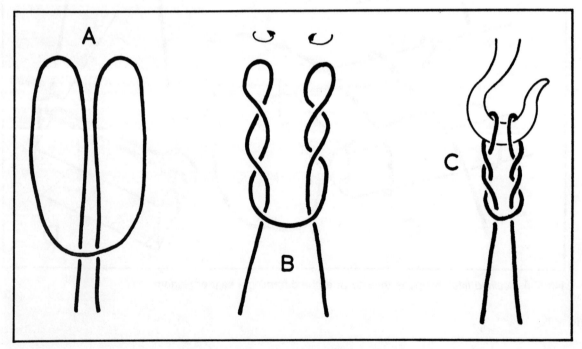

Fig. 7-6. The twisted loops of a *catspaw* attach a rope to a hook (A,B,C).

a clove hitch may slide on a smooth or slippery pole. It is really a clove hitch with an extra turn. Start as if making a clove hitch, but go around twice (Fig. 7-7A), then go over both turns and continue in the same direction around the pole to make the final half hitch (Fig. 7-7B). This hitch can be used in any of the same applications as a clove hitch and, like that hitch, should have loads on both ends. A half hitch might be put around the standing part for improved security, if you use the magnus hitch for a temporary end fastening (Fig. 7-2H).

Another use for the magnus hitch at sea was for attaching a sail with a grommet or eyelet at its edge to a spar, and this may have applications in ropework ashore. The sail had a line spliced into the eyelet. This was taken round the spar and back through the eye (Fig. 7-7C), then round again and over both turns (Fig. 7-7D) to make the finishing half hitch (Fig. 7-7E).

A clove hitch or magnus hitch is intended for a load across a pole. The rolling hitch is for a load along a pole or a thicker rope. The magnus hitch can be identified by having one part crossing two turns. The rolling hitch has two parts over one turn.

To make a rolling hitch, have the standing part coming from the load and use the working end to go around twice over it (Fig. 7-8A). Continue around in the same direction to finish with the usual half hitch (Fig. 7-8B).

That is all that may be needed to take a temporary load in the direction of the spar, whether you want to lift a weight vertically or pull something along a horizontal spar. For greater security, the working end may be taken around the pole or rope and seized to it (Fig. 7-8C). The seizing is not there to take the load, only to keep the final half hitch tight.

On a sailing ship a light pulley tackle, called a "handy billy," was provided with rope tails at each end. To assist in pulling a large rope or hawser tight, this was secured at one end to a point on the deck, then the other tail attached temporarily to the hawser, so the handy billy could be used to help pull it. Something similar may have other applications today.

The tail to the hawser was attached with a rolling hitch, not always completed, so it could be moved along as progress was made. The end from a fully formed rolling hitch may be gripped by hand instead of seized (Fig. 7-8D). A sufficient temporary grip might be obtained by leaving out the last half hitch and merely holding the end (Fig. 7-8E). Taking the end around is important for a frictional grip, particularly if you are dealing with smooth synthetic rope.

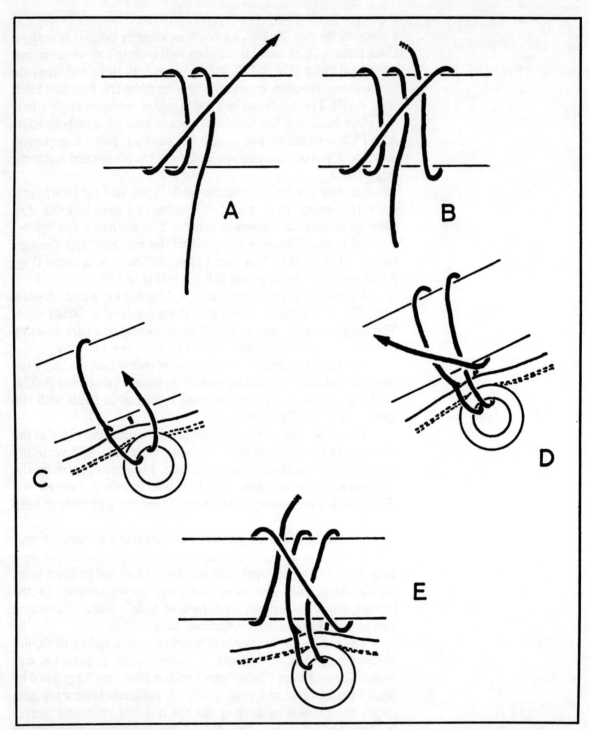

Fig. 7-7. In the *magnus hitch,* one more turn than a clove hitch gives extra grip (A,B). Another version attaches eyeletted canvas to a spar (C,D,E).

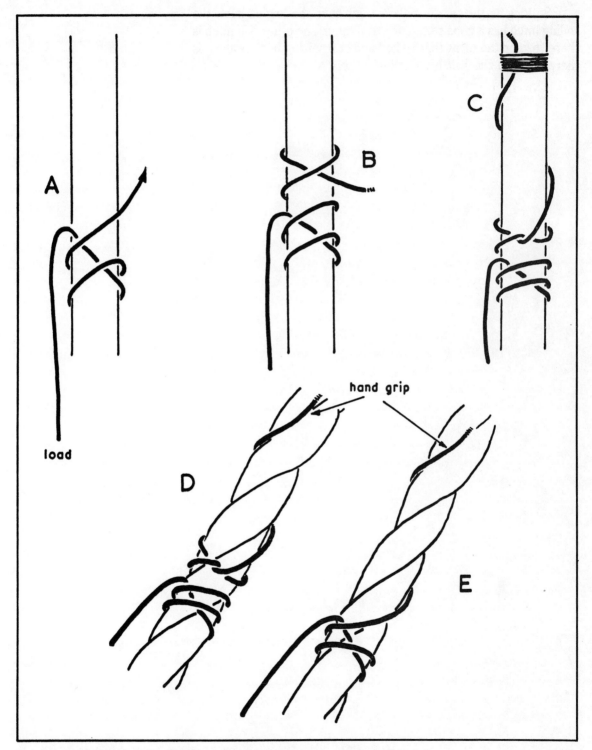

Fig. 7-8. *Rolling hitch* is for attaching a load to a spar or a thicker rope.

So long as the two turns are tight over the loaded part, the rolling hitch has a good resistance to sliding. The other half hitch is there to keep the turns tight. The hand or a seizing further along is there to keep the half hitch doing its job.

Chapter 8

Knots That Tighten

A frequent need in knotting is for a means of tightening and securing a cord round a parcel, bag, bundle of rods, or to gather together other loose items. Quite often the line is just string, which may be cut and discarded, so the knot does not have to be easy to untie. For larger wrappings, the line would be rope and you need to be able to undo the knot so the rope is available for further use.

Some of the joining knots may be used where maximum tightening is unnecessary. The reef knot is used in bandaging, and it could be used on some parcels. The first half can be held so it does not slip by pressing a finger on it while the second twists are made, but this does not allow tightening to the extent possible with other knots described here. The sheet bend or any other knot where one part has to be woven round the other are not parcel knots.

A knot for string on a parcel that has to be drawn tight has to be made as a slip knot that can be locked. One form is a *figure eight slip knot,* which has been given many names, but is here called a *packer's knot.* With the ends of the line brought together over the parcel, take the working end and make a figure eight knot around the other part so it finishes with line standing up a short distance (Fig. 8-1A). It is less satisfactory if twisted the other way. Pull the other part to tighten the wrapping. There will be enough friction in the knot to hold while you complete by turning a half

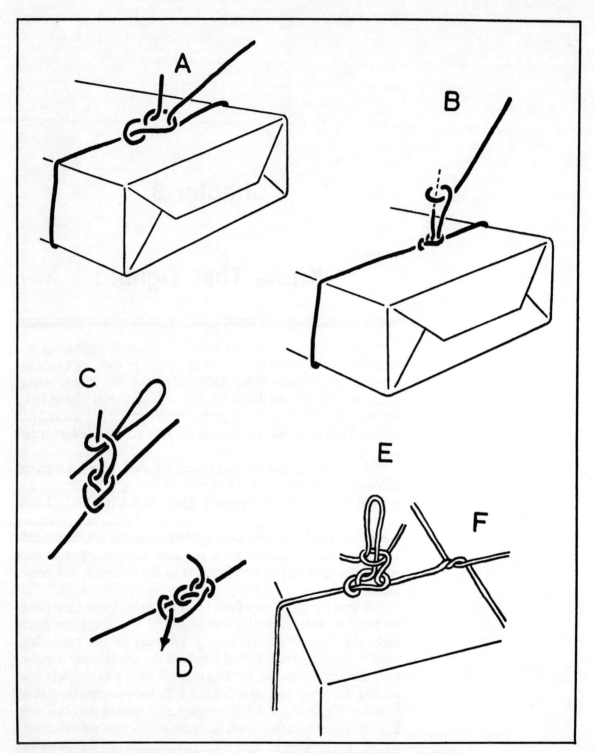

Fig. 8-1. *Packer's knot* tightens string around a parcel, then is locked with a half hitch.

hitch over the upstanding end (Fig. 8-1B). This locks the knot, and you cut off the excess ends.

It is possible to start with an overhand knot, but the extra twist of a figure eight is preferable. If you want to be able to release the knot, make the half hitch with a bight (Fig. 8-1C) so you can pull its end. Alternatively, make the half hitch over the opposite part (Fig. 8-1D), preferably with a bight. A third way is to turn back the upstanding part, so the half hitch goes around its bight (Fig. 8-1E). In each case, pulling the end from the bight allows the knot to be loosened or undone completely, while tension around the package remains until then.

If you take string two or more ways around a parcel, twist the crossing parts together (Fig. 8-1F) or make a clove hitch with one on the other. If you double the string for extra strength, clove hitches over two strings are advisable at every place where they cross.

The packer's knot may be used, but is not so satisfactory, for drawing tight the neck of a bag or sack. For that purpose there is a *constrictor knot,* which deserves to be better known. This knot, and variations of it, have been used by millers and other users of sacks, yet it was not recorded in early knotting books probably because their writers were seamen and the knot was not known on board ships.

It is also useful as a temporary whipping, as when you are about to cut a stranded rope that may unlay as soon as the ends are released. If you cut between two constrictor knots, they will hold the new ends tight. This is a knot to be made in string, rather than rope. It is usual to cut the string after using this knot, although there are versions which can be released.

Put a turn rather like the start of a clove hitch on the neck of the bag, or whatever it is to be drawn together (Fig. 8-2A). Take the working end around the under turn in an overhand knot (Fig. 8-2B), going out below the outer turn. Pull the ends to tighten so the overhand knot is trapped under the outer turn (Fig. 8-2C). As the overhand knot is tightened, the outer turn is also tightened to lock on it. This should be satisfactory for most bags and sacks, but if the amount of fabric being constricted is large in relation to the string, you can put on an extra turn (Fig. 8-2D). If you want to be able to release the knot, make the overhand knot with a bight (Fig. 8-2E), but even then a really tight closure may resist undoing.

If you have to pull together a bundle of logs or branches, neither of the previous knots will function for tightening, although

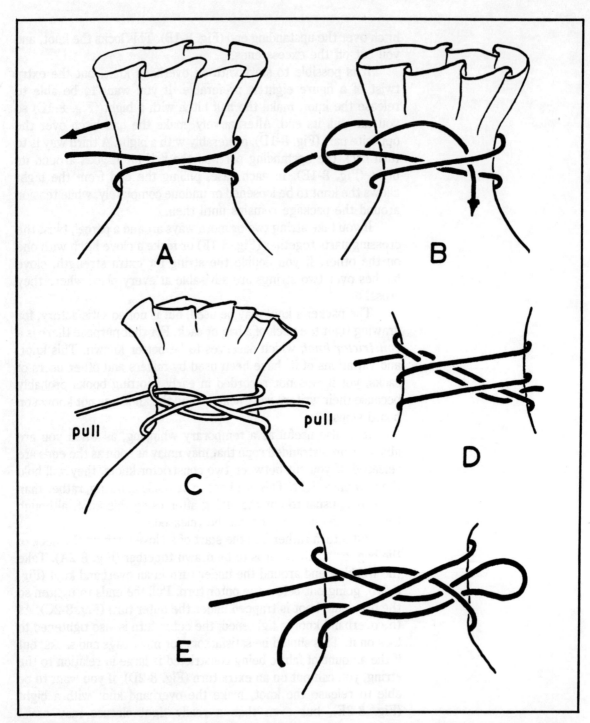

Fig. 8-2. *Constrictor knot* tightens and locks (A,B,C). It can be doubled (D) or a bight may be tucked (E).

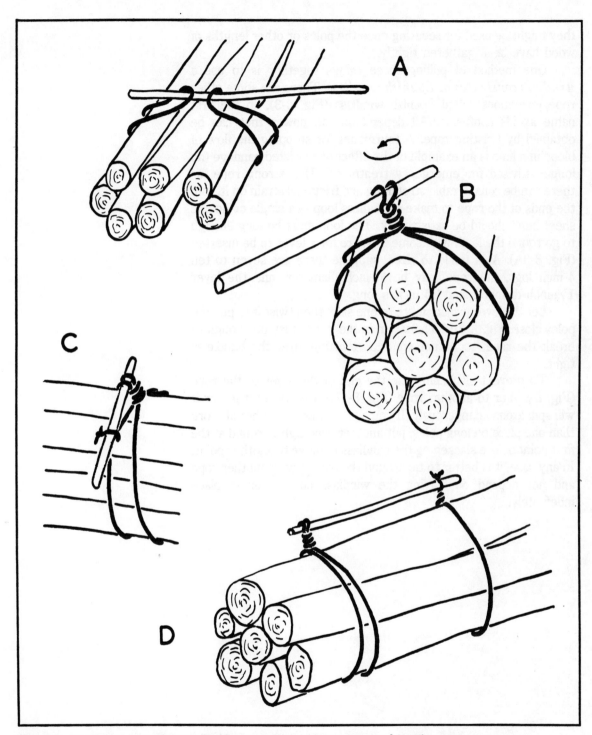

Fig. 8-3. A *windlass constrictor* pulls things together with tne power of twisting rope.

they might be used for securing once the poles or other lengths of wood have been gathered tightly.

One method of pulling these things together is to use a *windlass constrictor* or *Spanish windlass*. There are some other rope formations called Spanish windlass (Fig. 8-3), so the first name avoids confusion. All depend on the power that can be obtained by twisting rope. A tourniquet for stopping the flow of blood in a limb is an example of the effect of a twisted bandage (no longer advised for emergency treatment). Use strong rope, as there can be considerable stretching and frictional strain on it. Join the ends of the rope to make an endless loop—a single or double sheet bend should be satisfactory. The loop must be long enough to go round the load, with some to spare for a lever to be inserted (Fig. 8-3A). As a guide to sizes, suppose there are seven to ten 4-inch logs, the rope may be ½-inch diameter, and the lever 1½-inch diameter and 30 inches long.

Let the lever project more to one side, then twist it to pull the poles close (Fig. 8-3B). The strain in the twists may be enough to break the rope, so do not continue twisting after the bundle is tight.

To prevent slackening, tie the end of the lever to the rope (Fig. 8-3C) or to another rope (Fig. 8-3D). Do not let it go, or it will spin around dangerously. If you have to draw together at more than one place on long poles, put another rope tightly round at the first point before slackening the windlass to move to another point. In any case, it is better to tie around the bundle with another rope and not depend on leaving the windlass constrictor in place indefinitely.

Chapter 9

Knots for Shortening Rope

If a piece of rope is too long between two points, it can often be brought to the right length by taking up the slack at one end and reknotting there. In many circumstances, that is the best way of dealing with the problem. At other times, you may have to gather up the slack without untying the ends. This may happen if shortening is only a temporary measure and you want to restore the full length later.

The basic knot for this purpose is the *sheepshank* (Fig. 9-1A), which is made without using the ends of the rope. Gather the slack into a long S-shape (Fig. 9-1B). Twist a half hitch in the rope near one end and slip it over the bight there (Fig. 9-1C). Be careful not to twist the other way. Make a half hitch in the same way at the other end and push the bight through it (Fig. 9-1D). If you need to get the maximum tension in the knotted rope, instead of making the second half hitch in the single line, use the end of that bight to twist over the standing part (Fig. 9-1E) and pull it hard outwards so the half hitch is forced into the tensioned single line and the bight is the same as the other end (Fig. 9-1F).

As long as a sheepshank is under a steady tension, it is secure, but if the rope alternates between slack and tight, it may come apart. One way of reducing this risk is to put a piece of wood across each end (Fig. 9-1G). It could be seized in place, but a more secure way is to seize the loops to the standing parts at each end (Fig. 9-1H).

If you want to make the knot itself more secure and avoid

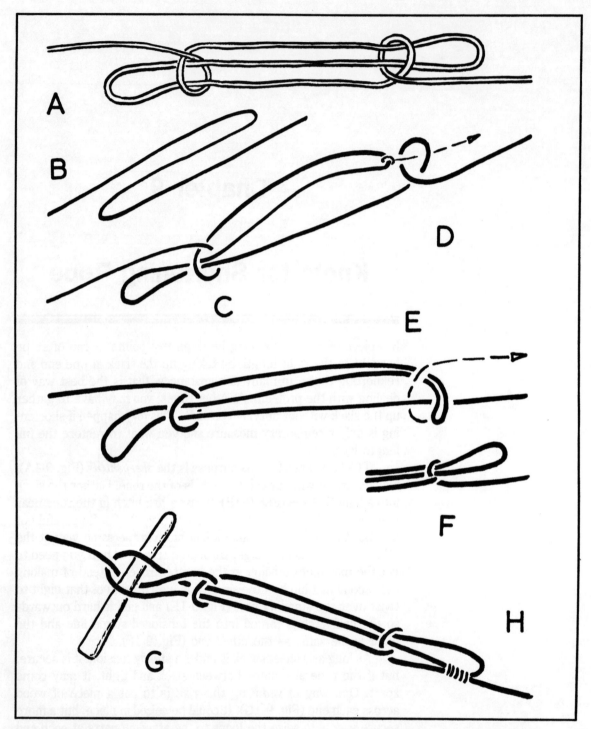

Fig. 9-1. *Sheepshank* (A) is for shortening rope (B,C,D). It can be made tightly (E,F) and locked (G,H).

additions or using the ends of the rope, the sheepshank can be converted into a *dogshank*. Instead of a half hitch at each end, form the loop as if making an overhand knot, but instead of pulling the end through, pass the bight across (Fig. 9-2A). Do this at both ends (Fig. 9-2B). Tuck through as shown and the knot will lock. If you form the partial overhand knot the other way, the pull does not come on the twist and may slip when the rope slackens. What you have formed at each end are *lever* or *marline spike hitches* (Fig. 11-1).

There is a second use for both of these knots: they can strengthen a weak part in a rope. If the rope is frayed or there is other local weakening, make the long S-shape with the weak part at the center (Fig. 9-2C). When you complete a sheepshank or dogshank, the two parts on each side will take some of the load off the weak center (Fig. 9-2D). It is even possible to cut through at the center; while tension is maintained, the side pieces will take the load, but shaking the loosened rope will upset the knot.

If there is a large amount of rope to be gathered up you can avoid a very long sheepshank or dogshank by making up several loops with the slack. Half hitches may go over the ends, but if there are many turns it would be better to slip on a clove hitch, in the form of two half hitches (Fig. 9-2E). This should resist loosening in moderate slackening and tightening of the whole rope (Fig. 9-2F). You may also use clove hitches on the single S-shape of a sheepshank. Either way may be called a *clove hitched sheepshank*.

A variation of this knot is used for shortening a hanging rope, and it may be called a *bell ringer's knot* from its use in gathering up the slack in a church bell rope when it is out of use. Take up the amount of rope to be shortened. This may be anything from a single loop to a large number of turns. Put a half hitch over the top of the bundle (Fig. 9-2G), followed by another to complete a clove hitch (Fig. 9-2H). Draw the turns close together tightly near the top of the bundle (Fig. 9-2J).

Coiling rope for storage is a form of shortening. Large and long rope may have to be made into round coils then pieces of light line tied round at intervals. Thinner and more flexible rope in reasonable lengths can be coiled and locked for hanging or other storage with a hitch in itself. The size of the coil will depend on the length and diameter, but ½-inch diameter rope, for example, may be coiled in front of you with both hands so the loops are 15 to 20 inches long.

Make up the rope into coils all about the same size, with a piece of any length projecting from the last loop (Fig. 9-3A). Hold

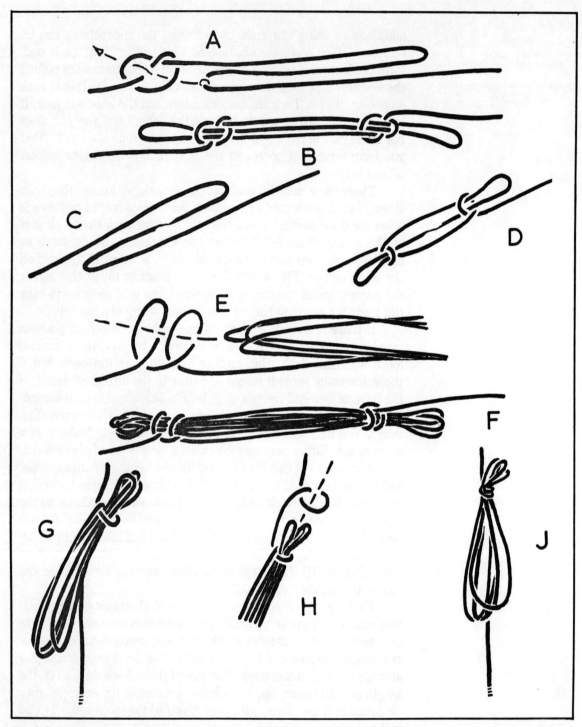

Fig. 9-2. *Dogshank* has more secure ends (A,B). Both knots will strengthen a weak part (C,D). More slack can be gathered in the same way (E–J).

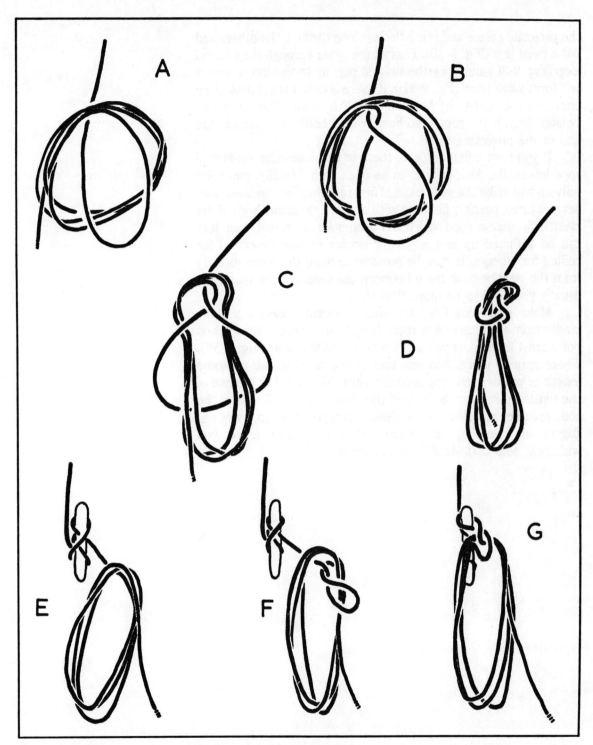

Fig. 9-3. A coil of rope may be secured with a twisted half hitch.

the projecting piece and bring the last loop through the others and put a twist in it (Fig. 9-3B). Pass all the other through the twisted loop (Fig. 9-3C) and draw the twisted part up to the top, where it will form a half hitch (Fig. 9-3D). If there is only a short projecting end, you can make the half hitch with it, instead of using the twisted loop. If the rope is to hang from a hook, tie a loop in the end of the projecting piece.

If you hoist a flag or a sail, there is a considerable amount of rope left on the deck or floor to be dealt with. Usually, you hoist fully up and make the rope halliard fast to a cleat on the mast with several turns, possibly finishing with a half hitch on one horn of the cleat. The excess rope which has accumulated around your feet can be gathered up in a way very similar to that described for coiling for storage. It may be possible to hang the loops directly from the cleat or push them between the rope and the mast, but usually you need to do more than that.

Make your coils from the cleat outwards, leaving a short length from the attachment there (Fig. 9-3E). Reach through and put a twist in the part you pull from next to the cleat (Fig. 9-3F). There may be more than one turn if you need to use up some length or you have to wrap around a very thick coil. Lift the end of the twisted part over the horn of the cleat (Fig. 9-3G) to hold the coils together and close to the cleat. When you want to lower the flag or sail, releasing the twisted part from the cleat leaves you with neat coils that should run out smoothly.

Chapter 10

Quick-Release Hitches

There are occasions when you want to secure something, yet be able to cast it off quickly. There must be no fear of the loaded end coming loose when it is not intended to, yet a pull on the other end must let the whole knot go instantaneously. There may be something hanging that you want to be able to drop. It could be a horse tethered to a post, rail, or ring that you want to be able to release by pulling a rope after you have mounted. It may be a boat moored to a dock, but which you do not wish to let go until you have started the outboard motor. You may be taking a tow with a trolley or a boat, but you want to be able to cast off quickly if anything goes wrong. The knot and its load could be some way from where you wait with the free end to let it go.

Some knots described earlier have versions where completion can be with a bight instead of an end, so pulling the end from the bight will loosen the knot, even if it does not completely dismantle it. Tying your shoe lace in a bow is a form of quick-release knot. Better quick-release knots bring the whole rope away as they are released, so there is no further action needed. Most of these knots are to something solid, although some would be effective around another rope.

The best-known quick-release knot is the *highwayman's hitch*. This was alleged to have been used to tether a horse in readiness for a quick getaway. After holding up and robbing a coach, the highwayman jumped on his horse, pulled the end of the halter and released the horse from the tree to which it had been tied. You may not have exactly that need, but it may well be your first choice when you need a hitch that is secure under load, yet has a positive release action. There has to be ample rope for a double length as securing is with a bight.

To make a highwayman's hitch, put a bight of rope behind the post or rail, or up through a ring (Fig. 10-1A). Identify what will be the loaded part and make sure the other part is long enough to reach to wherever you will be when you release it, allowing you to be quite a long way if that suits the circumstances, as when you want to drop the door of a trap when you are not near it.

Lift a bight of the part which will take the load and push it through the first bight, which is pulled to tighten on it (Fig. 10-1B). Now put a bight of the release rope through the second bight and pull on the loaded part to tighten it (Fig. 10-1C). That completes the knot, but make sure the bights are as tight as possible against the solid object. Settle the knot in shape before letting the loaded part take the strain.

To make that hitch, you have to work close to the pole or ring. Sometimes it is more convenient to form the quick-release part some way from the solid object. For instance, you may be mooring a boat to a dock when there is considerable rise and fall of tide, so the ring or bollard could be quite high. A variation of the highwayman's hitch still uses one bight to lock another, but the work of forming the locking bights can be done some way from the mooring point—you can sit in the boat instead of having to reach to a nearly impossible position to tuck bights.

Get a bight into position and bring it down alongside the part that will take the load, any distance that suits your convenience (Fig. 1-1D). Throw a ring in the standing part to put a half hitch over the end of the bight (Fig. 10-1E), in the same way as dealing with one end of a sheepshank. Pass a small bight of the free part across that bight to lock the standing part (Fig. 10-1F).

Adjust the bights so their crossings are close, and the parts coming from the mooring point are all about the same length. With this arrangement, you can manage single-handed in a boat in a fast-running tide. You can start the motor, then pull the rope end to cast off when you know that everything is under control.

Another advantage of this variation is that it can be used on a thin solid object, such as an iron peg or quite a slim ring. The highwayman's hitch is better on something thicker, such as a tree trunk, branch, stout post, or mooring bollard.

In the third variation, there are more turns to provide friction while holding the rope to a post or rail, which may be an advantage

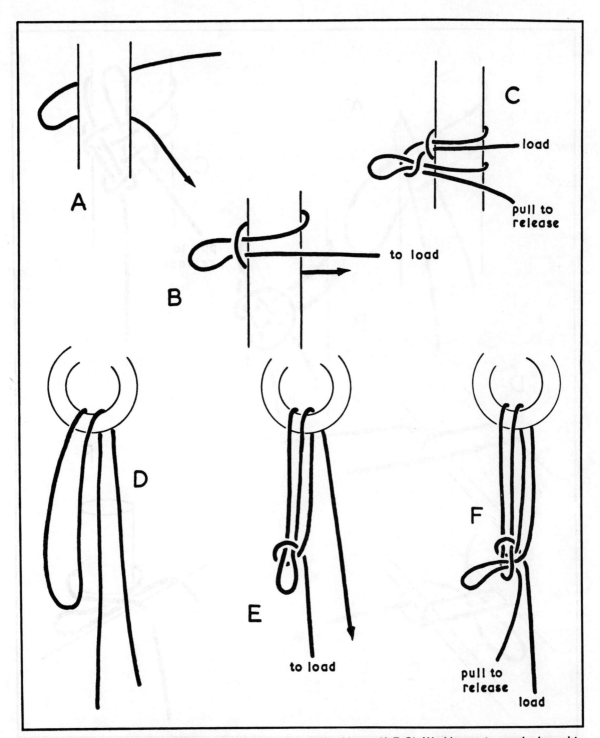

Fig. 10-1. In the *highwayman's hitch,* there are two interlocked loops (A,B,C). Working parts may be brought lower if more convenient (D,E,F).

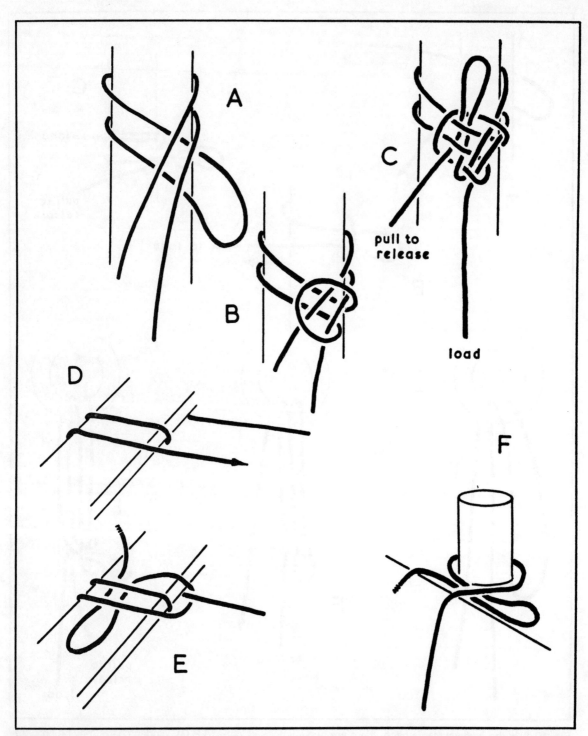

Fig. 10-2. This version of the highwayman's hitch has more turns for a better grip on a smooth surface (A,B,C). A slippery hitch uses a bight for quick release (D,E,F).

if there is a risk of slipping down or along, due to the spar being very smooth or oily or wet. This variation is not suitable for a ring.

Pass a bight round the spar, then under both parts (Fig. 10-2A). Double it back over itself (Fig. 10-2B). Tuck a bight from the release part over the main bight and under the turns on the spar (Fig. 10-2C). Adjust the hitch so it is tight on the spar and the main bight is close on the release one. A problem may come with this hitch if it has been under considerable load. The releasing bight may then be difficult to draw free.

A *slippery hitch* occurs when a bight is used to lock several turns. An example is an open boat being towed. If a small boat is towed at too great a speed, it could be pulled under, so if you are in the boat, you want to be able to cast off the tow line in an emergency. In this case, the rope from the towing craft is led through an eye or cleat at the stem of your boat to a thwart or other strong point.

Put a round turn on the thwart starting underneath (Fig. 10-2D). Take the working end under the standing part and use it to put a bight under the round turns (Fig. 10-2E). This will hold under load, but the tow rope will unwind and pull away when you jerk on the end from the bight. Even if there is no emergency, this allows you to rapidly disconnect when you get to your destination, as there are no turns of a knot to undo.

It is possible to use a slippery hitch for a temporary fastening in other circumstances. It is even used as the only fastening for some daredevil high flyers in South America. If there is a post or bollard a short distance back from an edge, a bight under the loaded part will hold under a downward steady strain (Fig. 10-2F). You can release it by pulling the free end or jerking the part that was loaded.

Chapter 11

Rope Power

Knotting nearly always means you are tightening a rope or cord. It may be string round a parcel, it could be a rope stretched to form a fence, you may want to hoist a load, or the rope has to be tightened to support a pole or tent. In all cases, you want at least a reasonable tension and quite often all the tension possible.

The obvious way to increase power for maximum tension is to use pulleys, but there are ways of using just the rope itself to pull tighter or lift more.

One problem is getting a grip on the line. If you can pull with a strong and comfortable hold, you can exert more power. String or cord is difficult to grip. You may wrap it around your hand, but that hurts when you pull. Even rope up to about ½-inch diameter is not easy to grip directly when you want to pull with all your strength. You can increase your grip and use two hands if necessary if you use a *lever hitch.*

The lever hitch is also known as a *marline spike hitch,* from the use of the spike which every seaman carried in the days of sailing ships. The spike was up to 12 inches long and used for many things, including opening the strands of rope for splicing. If made of wood, it may have been called a *fid.* You may not have one of these spikes, but you can use a piece of wood or metal as a handle. If you are dealing with string, it might be a pencil, but something thicker will be needed for rope.

The lever hitch is simple and temporary. You use it with a piece of wood to provide a grip while you pull, then withdraw the wood after tension has been applied and the hitch disappears. Start twisting the rope as if about to make an overhand knot (Fig. 11-1A). Instead of pulling through, push your handle across under what would have been pulled through (Fig. 11-1B). Arrange the twist so the handle will be pulled against the twist in the hitch (Fig. 11-1C). In some stiff line, the knot may hold without help, but usually you should grip over the hitch as you pull.

Besides the direct pull, this hitch can be used with a longer pole for levering. For instance, suppose there is a stubborn tent stake to be withdrawn. Fasten the end of a rope to the stake with a round turn and two half hitches, or other knot. Put a lever hitch on a light pole and lever that against the ground to pull the stake (Fig. 11-1D). If you arrange the lever so the length between the lever hitch and the ground end of the lever is much less than the distance to your hand (Fig. 11-1E), you will exert much more power on the rope than if the difference is not so great (Fig. 11-1F). This is a useful means of increasing the pull you give on a rope under many circumstances, such as tightening a lashing.

When rope is used with pulleys, the resulting assembly is called a *tackle* (which a seaman pronounces "tayckle"). The pulleys are enclosed in *blocks*. The use of blocks and tackle is outside the scope of this book, but there are ways of using similar principles with rope only. In many assemblies of blocks and tackle, there is a mechanical advantage, meaning you apply a certain power and this is increased by the tackle into increased power applied to the load. There is always some loss due to friction, but if the pulleys, or *sheaves*, are large and on good bearings, this may be slight. If you try to use similar means with rope pulling over rope, the loss due to friction may be so great as to cancel out any mechanical advantage, so a *rope tackle* can only be simple, to have minimum friction.

If you take a rope through a block with a single sheave that is hanging from a beam (Fig. 11-2A), you only alter the direction of the rope, without any increase in power. If that block is attached to the load and one end of the rope is secured, pulling on the other end draws the block and load towards you, and you have a mechanical advantage of two to one (Fig. 11-2B). You will apply a load while only exerting an effort about equal to half that, but the load will only move half the distance you haul on the rope. There is a commonly used rope tackle that has a comparable action. Despite losses by friction, there is still an appreciable gain. One application is in drawing tight a rope over a load on the back of a truck.

To use a rope tackle, make sure there is ample spare rope

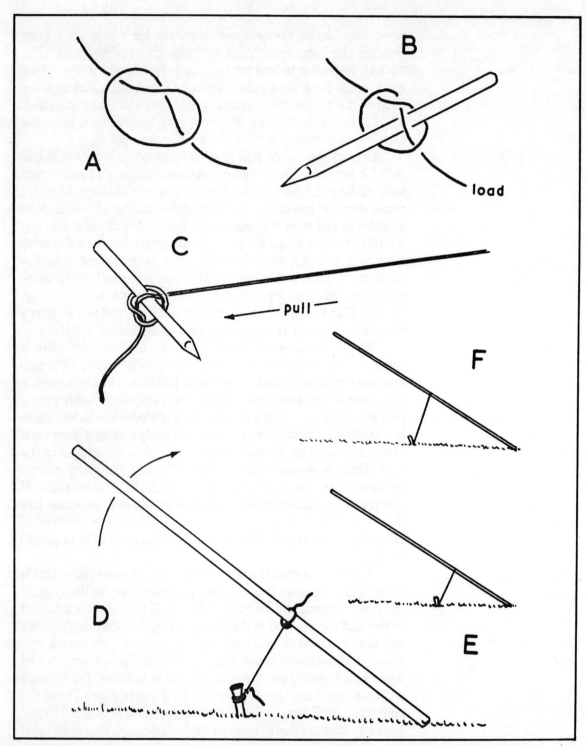

Fig. 11-1. *Lever hitch* (A,B,C) gives a quick temporary grip or purchase for pulling or levering (D,E,F).

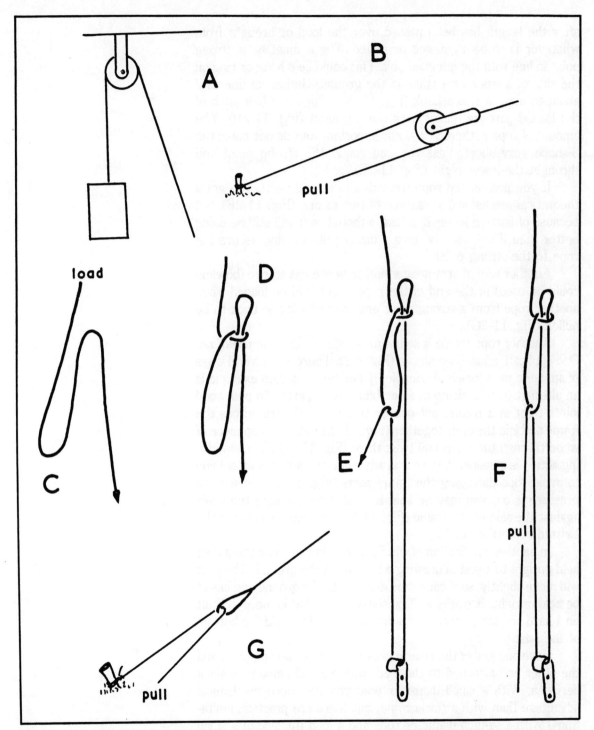

Fig. 11-2. A pulley may alter direction of the rope (A) or provide a purchase (B). A rope tackle has the same effect (C–G).

after the length has been passed over the load or brought from whatever is to be tightened or pulled. There must be a strong point in line with the intended pull. This could be a hook or ring on the side of a truck or a stake in the ground. Gather up line as if about to make a sheepshank (Fig. 11-2C). Turn in a half hitch of the loaded part and put it over the top bight (Fig. 11-2D). The amount of rope gathered up is not important, but do not make the S-shape very short. Pass the end round the strong point and throught the lower bight (Fig. 11-2E).

If you pull on the rope towards the strong point, you get a theoretical mechanical advantage of two to one (Fig. 11-2F), but because of friction losses it is less, although you will still be doing better than if you merely gave a direct pull. Finally, secure the rope to the strong point.

Another way of arranging a similar tackle has an eye (bowline could be used) in the end of the rope which will be loaded, then another rope from a strong point goes through it and back to be pulled (Fig. 11-2G).

Another rope tackle is sometimes called a *Spanish windlass.* One application has been shown (Fig. 8-3). There are several ways of applying the tension obtainable by twisting rope. An example is an alternative to a clamp in assembling wood parts. To pull wood joints tight in a frame, put one or two turns of cord across the frame and join the ends together (Fig. 11-3A). Put a scrap piece of wood through the turns and twist them (Fig. 11-3B). The squeezing action is considerable, so it is advisable to have blocks outside to avoid rope damaging the frame parts (Fig. 11-3C). When the pressure is on, you may be able to lock it by jamming the lever against the side of the frame (Fig. 11-3D), or you could tie to the twisted rope (Fig. 11-3E).

In another application of the Spanish windlass, you use a post held upright to assist in drawing a load along the ground. The post will move slightly, so it cannot be driven into the ground and has to be held upright. It works well on soil or grass, but is more difficult on a hard smooth surface. Extra help is needed to hold the bottom of the post.

Have one end of the rope anchored to a fixed strong point and the other end attached to the load, with a small amount of slack between. With a small diameter post you get more mechanical advantage than with a thicker one, but there are practical limitations. With a ½-inch diameter rope and a load the size of a small car, a post about 3 inches diameter is suitable. Twist a turn of the rope around a lever (Fig. 11-3F) and wind this around the post

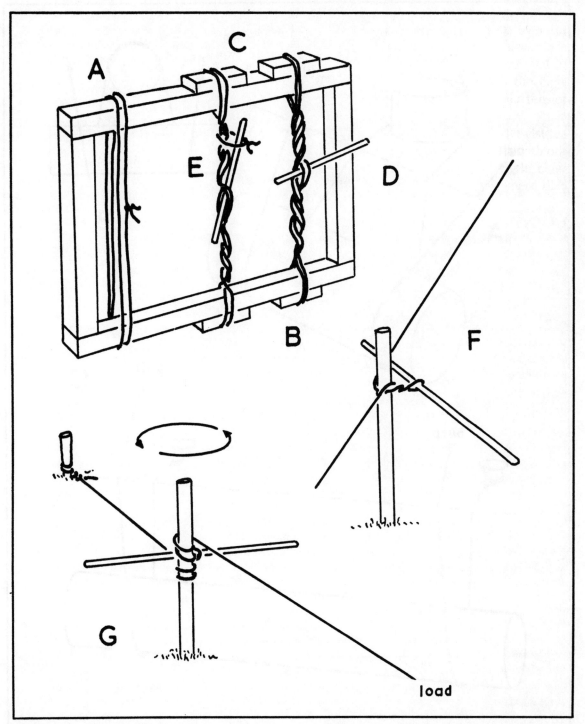

Fig. 11-3. *Spanish windlass* will act as a clamp (A–E), or another version makes a powerful hauling windlass (F,G).

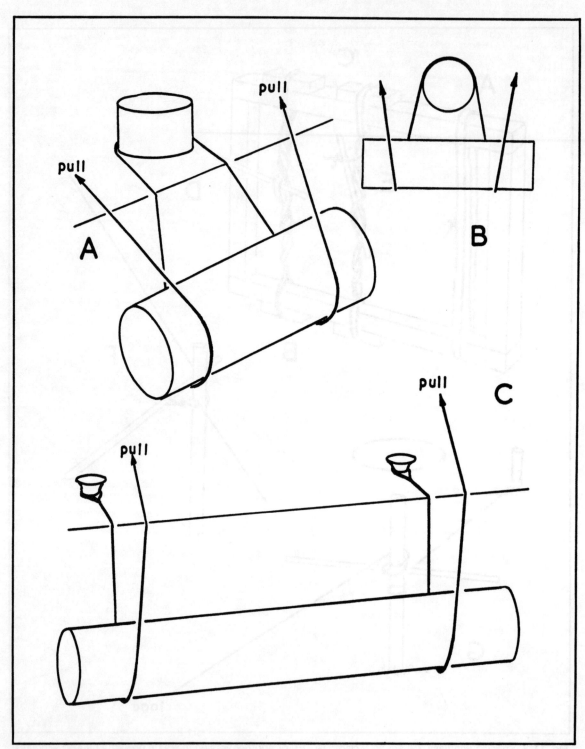

Fig. 11-4. A *parbuckle* will roll and lift a round object.

between the line from the anchorage and the part to the load (Fig. 11-3G). Steady the top of the post while you twist the lever around it several times. The effect is to exert considerable power, but the load does not move much with each turn. Because of the progressive tilt of the post and build-up of rope turns, you will have to chock the load and shorten the rope to repeat the process as often as necessary to move the load as far as you wish.

A way of shifting something that will roll is called a *parbuckle*. This does not involve frictional losses of any appreciable amount. You can roll a log, drum of oil, or anything else cylindrical along the ground, up a slope, or vertically up a wall or the side of a ship. If the round item is not very long, you may use one rope and pull from a single strong point, but you get better control if you use two ropes and widely spaced anchorage points.

For a single point and a short load, loop the rope around the strong point, or secure it there with a clove hitch, then take the ends under the load and back to be pulled (Fig. 11-4A). Have an assistant, so you both pull slightly outwards and can keep the rolling cylinder straight (Fig. 11-4B). Pulling towards the center may cause it to roll out of line.

With two ropes and two strong points, you can move something like a log of any length (Fig. 11-4C), with direct pulls. If it is a heavy load moving vertically, you should have helpers taking up the slack and ready to secure the hauling ropes to the strong point whenever you stop pulling, so the log cannot roll back.

Chapter 12

Sliding Knots

Sometimes it is useful to have a knot that can be adjusted by sliding yet has enough friction to hold a load. It is obviously unwise to depend only on friction in dangerous situations or when a heavy load must be held without a risk of moving or falling. A sliding knot with only a frictional hold has uses in a temporary situation or when frequent adjustment of a fairly light load will be expected. Some sliding knots can be locked after they have been adjusted, using a half hitch or an additional knot. An example of this, already described, is the packer's knot (Fig. 8-1). However, where a secure hold is required, and there is no need for the adjustment given by a sliding knot, it is better to use one of the more positive knots.

A guyline for a tent is often provided with a wood or metal slider, which holds in any position by friction on the slightly kinked rope. Knots can be arranged to have a similar effect in this or similar conditions. Climbers sometimes need a knot which will slide and hold temporarily, then can be moved to a new position to hold again as they process upwards or downwards under control. Fishermen have uses for sliding knots. Besides those which can be locked with extra hitches, they have devised some that will slide until you distort them, then they take a different formation, which should not move under load.

For a guyline situation, or anywhere you want to adjust and take a light load, there are knots based on the overhand knot. A middleman's knot or fisherman's loop (Fig. 6-1) can be put around a stake and adjustment made by sliding the overhand knots closer or further apart (Fig. 12-1A). There is only a limited adjustment, but if you start with a long loop there is more rope to move. If the overhand knots are kept tight, there should be enough friction to allow sliding when you want to move them and a grip when released.

For a simple variation on this there is a *guyline hitch* (Fig. 12-1B). Make two overhand knots in the main part of the rope, leaving a tail long enough for your needs. Keep the knots open and a reasonable distance apart — 12 inches on ⅜-inch rope should be satisfactory. Pass the tail end down through the knots. Going into the knot the same way as the standing part (Fig. 12-1C) is neatest, but you get slightly more grip by angling the rope, if you go in from the other side (Fig. 12-1D). Tightening is by pulling through more of the tail. If you want to lock the knot at any position, tie an overhand or figure-eight knot in the tail near the end knot (Fig. 12-1E).

For a variation on this, use only one overhand knot in the main line, then take the tail through this and make an overhand knot with it around the standing part (Fig. 12-1F). In effect, you are making a fisherman's knot. This has comparable frictional hold to the previous version, but it is not so easily locked if you need to secure it at a particular setting.

If the rope you are using is very smooth or has become slippery because of moisture, you can increase friction in one or both parts of these knots by doubling the turns in the overhand knot, as in the double fisherman's knot (Fig. 3-3E). It is advisable to check the action with single overhand knots first, because you may find adjustments difficult to make with double knots.

With the change to synthetic ropes, mountaineers have had to alter their ideas on knotting and experiment with new sliding knots, which are needed at some stages of a climb. Some of their sliding knots are adaptable to other rope uses. It should be remembered that a mountaineer's sliding knot is for use with rope on rope, and it may not be so successful if you try it with a rope on a pole. In any case, the rope used for the sliding knot must be much thinner than the rope it is attached to, and that rope must be under at least a moderate strain, although it need not be stretched rigidly.

The basic climber's sliding arrangement is a *Prusik knot,* named after the mid-European deviser. It is made with a continuous loop or *strop.* This might be a rope with its ends spliced together, but in a climbing situation it is more likely to be made

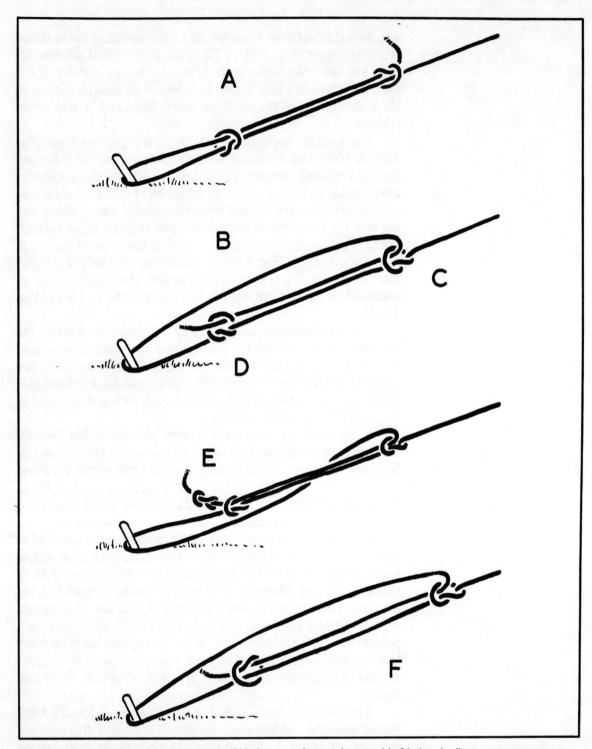

Fig. 12-1. Several ways of applying two half hitches may be used to provide frictional adjustment on guy ropes.

from one of the ropes which a climber carries around his waist, by tying the ends together. Current advice is to join the ends with a double fisherman's knot, despite its rather bulky form.

Take a part of the strop around the main rope (Fig. 12-2A), then round again, inside the first turns (Fig. 12-2B), taking care not to cross any parts. Pull through all you have wrapped on the main rope, so the other part tightens over it (Fig. 12-2C). That completes the knot. The load comes on the hanging loop and slightly distorts the main rope, so there is enough friction to grip. When the load is released, you can put your hand over the whole knot and slide it to a new position.

In practice, two Prusik knotted strops may be used, particularly in a long climb up a rope. You support yourself on one while moving the other to a new position. A climber may only have one hand free to make a Prusik knot, so he should practice forming it with one hand while hanging from the other.

Much use is made of *karabiners* by climbers. These are metal loops or coupling links with screw or other closures. There is a variation of the Prusik knot, which may also be called a *Bachmann knot,* which employs a karabiner. Use a continuous strop or a rope joined with a fisherman's knot, much thinner than the main rope and a standard screwgate karabiner.

Hook the strop onto the karabiner and lock its closure. Take the strop around the main rope and into the karabiner (Fig. 12-2D), then round again and let the excess hang (Fig. 12-2E). When there is a weight on the loop, there is enough friction to prevent slipping, but when the load is released, it is claimed that this variation is easier to move than the Prusik knot. It also works better on icy or wet ropes. It is probably a little easier to tie one-handed.

There is a long-standing use for the basic Prusik knot, which has nothing to do with sliding, and dates from seafaring days before the climbing use was devised. This is the method of attaching a strop to a horizontal spar or pole, so a tackle or any other load can be suspended (Fig. 12-2F).

Another named knot familiar to climbers is the *Tarbuck knot,* which is no longer favored by experts. This is an adjustable loop intended to join to a karabiner or used in a similar situation, but a figure-eight-on-a-bight is suggested by the experts instead of this.

Fishermen have devised several adjustable knots, mostly for forming loops in the end of line. Some rely on many turns, in the same way as a Tarbuck knot, but others get a final lock by altering the shape of the knot. One of these is the *crabber's knot,* which

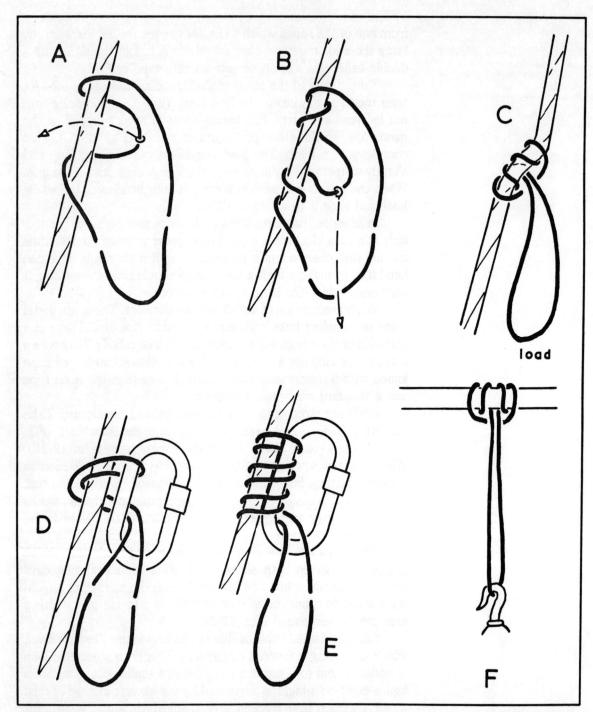

Fig. 12-2. *Prusik knot* is used by climbers as an adjustable support on another rope (A,B,C). Another version uses a *karabiner* (D,E). The Prusik knot is the same as the method of using a strop to hang a load from a spar (F).

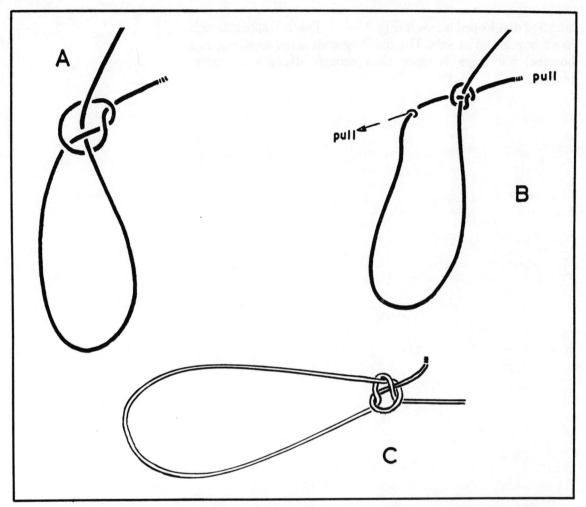

Fig. 12-3. *Crabber's knot* allows a loop to be adjusted (A), then the knot is distorted by pulling (B), so it takes a locked form (C).

may also be called a *crossed running knot*. It is intended to make a loop in the end of reasonably flexible rope, with the size set after you have adjusted the loop as you want it.

With the end, make turns almost the same as an overhand knot to enclose the standing part and trap it across the knot (Fig. 12-3A). Leave enough end extended so it cannot work back through the finished knot. Make the formation to form a loop of about the size you want, but you may adjust later to any size.

When you have the loop to the size you want, pull the end and the side of the loop opposite it in opposite directions (Fig. 12-3B). This will force the parts you are pulling into a small ring, with the standing part looped across it (Fig. 12-3C). The final appearance is like a bowline on its side. The resulting knot is not as strong as a bowline, but there is more than enough strength for many purposes.

Chapter 13

Joining Straps and Tapes

Flat material, such as leather straps and woven tapes, cannot be joined satisfactorily with knots intended for rope and cord. If tape or braid is very soft, it might be pulled into an approximately round section and joined with a rope knot, but this distorts the material for some distance each side of the knot, which may or may not matter. With light flexible cotton tape, such as is used for tying the neck of a bag, a simple reef bow may be made as easily as in cord and there is no need for any other knot.

With stiffer and thicker braid or tape, such as may be found on sports equipment, climbing gear, and heavier fabric assemblies, common rope knots are mostly unsuitable. This applies even more to leather thongs and straps, particularly wider ones which are used on horse and other harness.

On mountaineering equipment there are tapes with a construction that makes them fairly rigid in their cross-section, so any joining knot has to allow for the fact that they cannot be altered much in their width or thickness. The expert recommendation is for a *climber's tape knot*, which is a form of interleaved overhand knots, in which twisting of the tape is avoided.

Bring the ends together. Leave one end flat, and work the other end around it (Fig. 13-1A). Tuck that into an overhand knot, without twisting it, so the end rests along the standing part of the other piece (Fig. 13-1B). Take the second end back around the knot the other way (Fig. 13-1C) until the end extends along the opposite standing part (Fig. 13-1D). As you pull the knot tight, see

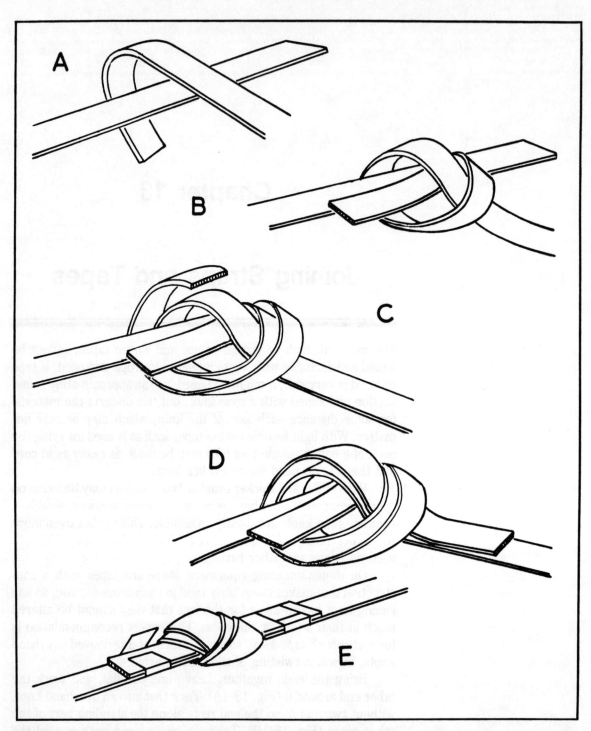

Fig. 13-1. The climber's *tape knot* is an interlocking form of two overhand knots, with one following round the other.

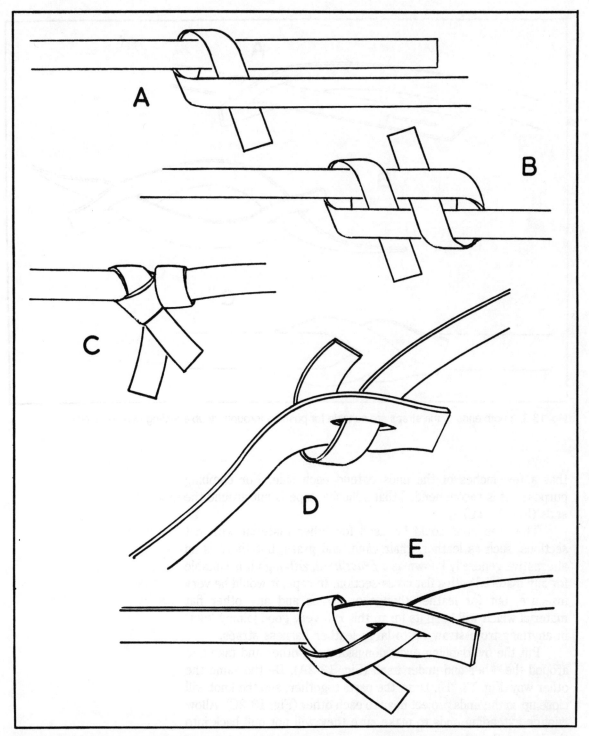

Fig. 13-2. *Grass knot* is a simple way to join straps (A,B,C). With stout leather, one part may be slit (D,E).

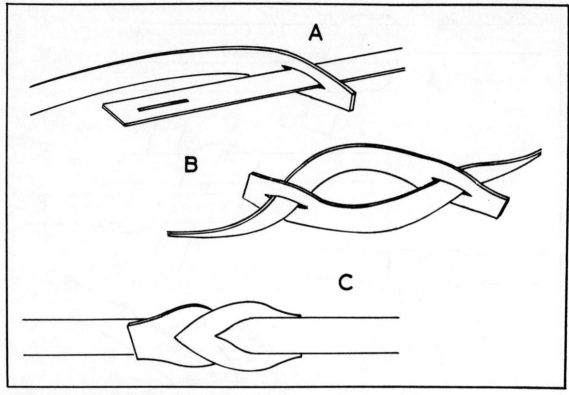

Fig. 13-3. If both ends of the straps are suitable for pushing through, double slitting can be used.

that a few inches of the ends extend each side. For climbing purposes, it is recommended that adhesive tape is put around the ends (Fig. 13-1E).

The tape knot could be used for other material with flat sections, such as leather, chair cane, and grass, but there is an alternative generally known as a *grass knot,* although it is suitable for any material with a flat cross-section. In rope, it would be very insecure, but for leather thongs or straps and any other flat material which will keep its form, this is a very good joining knot, in anything from straw up to large leather harness straps.

Put the overlapping ends alongside each other and take one around the other and under itself (Fig. 13-2A). Do the same the other way (Fig. 13-2B). Draw the parts together, and the knot will close up so the ends project near to each other (Fig. 13-2C). Allow enough extending ends to make sure they will not pull back into the knot under strain.

With stout leather, it is possible to slit a strap without fear of the opening extending under load. A variation of the grass knot uses a slit in one piece. Cut a slit long enough for the other end to pass through, far enough from its end for there to be enough strength in the remaining piece. Pass the second end through the slit, around the back (Fig. 13-2D) and across the front under itself (Fig. 13-2E).

Harness straps are usually attached to buckles or other parts which make those further ends unavailable when making a repair with a knot. In that case, either of the above knots can be used. If one or both ends are free and without anything attached that would add to their size, it is possible to join with slits in both ends.

Make slits with a good clearance. Slide one strap over the other (Fig. 13-3A) and pass its end through the other slit (Fig. 13-3B). With most leather, it is possible to manipulate the tightened join so both parts are flat and neat (Fig. 13-3C).

Chapter 14

Lashings

If you want to join spars or poles together, the ropework involved is calling *lashing*. At one time, all scaffolding for work on buildings, often of considerable height, was made by lashing poles together. In the Western World this has given way to steel tubing held together with screwed fittings, but in many countries, scaffolding is still made with ropes and poles. There will always be a need for skill in lashing poles together in frontier situations or in primitive conditions where structures have to be erected using facilities and materials at hand.

Fewer people in this country make use of poles lashed for professional purposes, but there will always be the enthusiastic amateurs in backwoods stiuations that get a tremendous satisfaction out of building bridges, towers, and similar things from poles and rope. If these structures are to be strong and safe, it is important that all lashings are properly made. A slipping lashing on a structure supporting several people could be disastrous. Fortunately, the skill needed to lash properly is easily acquired.

If a structure, whether of lashed poles or bolted steel strips, is to do its job, there are a few simple engineering principles which must be understood. The most important one is that you cannot push a triangle out of shape. If you join four poles or rods and a load comes at one corner, the assembly can be distorted (Fig. 14-1A). If you join three rods (Fig. 14-1B), there is no way the shape of the assembly can alter. From this we learn that a structure should be divided into triangles. If you put a diagonal across

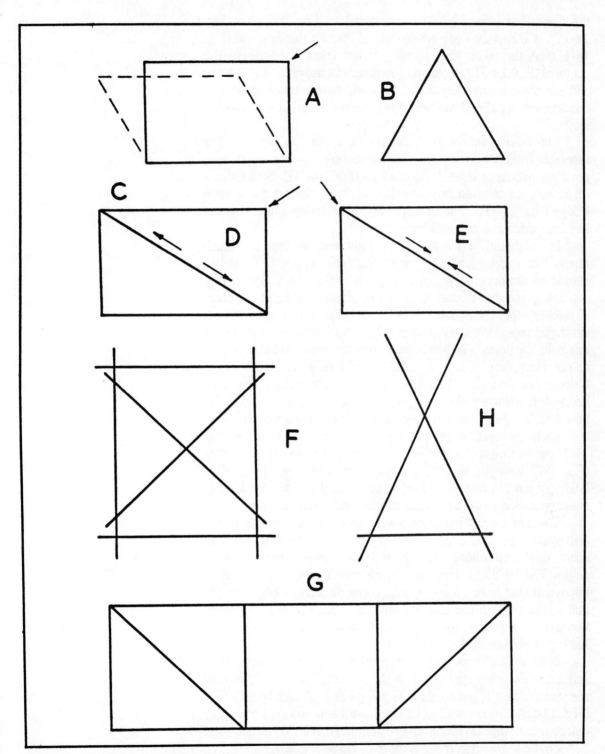

Fig. 14-1. Any structure is prevented from distorting by dividing its design into triangles.

the four-sided assembly, it is converted to two triangles (Fig. 14-1C). A thrust on one corner tries to stretch the diagonal (Fig. 14-1D). A thrust on the opposite corner tries to compress the diagonal (Fig. 14-1E). If you put diagonals both ways (Fig. 14-1F) and join them where they cross, they will have mutual support— the one trying to bend will be held by the one that has a stretching load.

The *triangulation principle* can be applied to anything you assemble from poles and rope. If the structure has four-sided bays, put diagonals in at least some of them (Fig. 14-1G). Some structures may be inherently triangular, as in a support for a rope bridge (Fig. 14-1H). The principle of triangulating applies even if the four sides are not parallel.

Poles should be reasonably straight and without too much taper. For regular use, the bark should be stripped off. Ropes should be comparatively thin in relation to the poles. Within reason, many turns of thinner rope will be stronger than fewer turns of thicker rope. Hairy natural fiber rope grips better than smooth synthetic rope. Avoid nylon and other ropes that stretch. As an example, for poles 3 inches in diameter, the rope could be ¼-inch or not more than ⅜-inch diameter. Avoid very stiff rope. Traditionally, the rope should be three-stranded, but braided rope may be used. If you are making a light ornamental structure with poles less than 2 inches diameter, any cord or thick string may be used.

Lashings must be tight, so a lever or marline spike hitch (Fig. 11-1) can be frequently used to pull or lever the line. Clove hitches (Fig. 7-2) have to be made, sometimes with one hand, while holding a tension with the other, so practice, if you are not already adept at making two half hitches under differing circumstances.

The *square lashing* is most commonly used. Anywhere that two spars cross and a load would try to make one slide over the other, this is the lashing, whether the poles cross squarely or at an angle. The lashing starts and finishes with clove hitches. It is important that their crossing parts come directly in line with the pull of the rope. A common mistake is to put the crossing some way around the spar, then it slips towards the pull later and the lashing is slackened.

Start with a clove hitch around the spar nearest to upright and under the other spar. Twist in the end (Fig. 14-2A). Go around the spars squarely, pulling tight as you go around each spar in turn (Fig. 14-2B). Do not wait until you have been around both spars before tensioning. Do not let the rope go diagonally on either spar.

Continue round in this way at least three times. Avoid letting

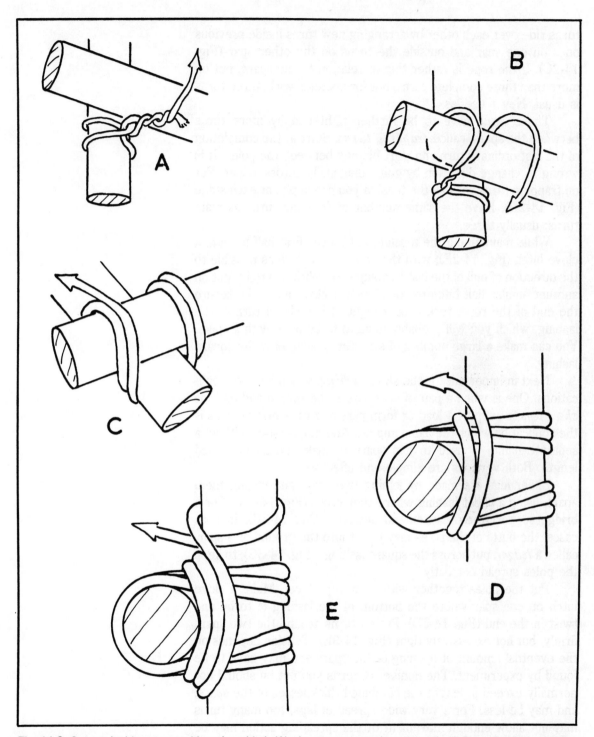

Fig. 14-2. *Square lashing* starts with a clove hitch (A), then turns are taken squarely (B,C), and tightened with *frapping turns* (D,E).

turns ride over each other by arranging new turns inside previous ones on one spar and outside the turns on the other spar (Fig. 14-2C). If the rope is rather thin in relation to the spars, put on more than three complete turns, but for average work, three turns is usual. Never use less.

These turns have to be further tightened by more turns between the spars, called *frapping turns.* Start at the completion of the last ordinary turn and start binding between the poles. It is wrong to change direction by going diagonally across a spar. Put on frapping turns with all the tension you can apply, at each stage (Fig. 14-2D). Have the same number of frapping turns as main turns; usually three.

While maintaining the tension, put on the first half hitch of a clove hitch (Fig. 14-2E), with the crossing as close as possible to the direction of pull of the last frapping turn. With this tight, put on another similar half hitch to complete the clove hitch. To secure the end of the rope, tuck it or a bight of it under a turn of the lashing, which you will probably have to force open with a spike, You can make a large number of structures using only the square lashing.

Next in importance is the *sheer lashing,* which has two applications. One is when a pair of spars are to be spread and used as *sheer legs* to support a load or form part of a rope bridge. This is the application which the name implies. Another version, without a separate name, is used to join spars to make up an increased length. Both versions are simple and effective.

Sheer legs are made by joining two spars and pulling them apart, using a sheer lashing where they cross (Fig. 14-3A). For a bridge support they may extend upwards (Fig. 14-3B). In both cases, the butts of the poles may be let into the ground or a spar, called a *ledger,* put across the square lashings (Fig. 14-3C), to keep the poles spread correctly.

Put the poles together with their tops level. Make a clove hitch on one spar where the bottom of the lashing is to be and twist in the end (Fig. 14-3D). Put on turns around the two spars firmly, but not excessively tight (Fig. 14-3E). Tension depends on the eventual amount of opening of the spars and may have to be found by experiment. The number of turns you put on should not normally exceed in length the combined thicknesses of the spars, and may be less. For a very wide spread of legs, too many turns may not allow enough movement or the spreading action may be enough to break the rope.

Open the legs slightly, while holding the tension on the rope.

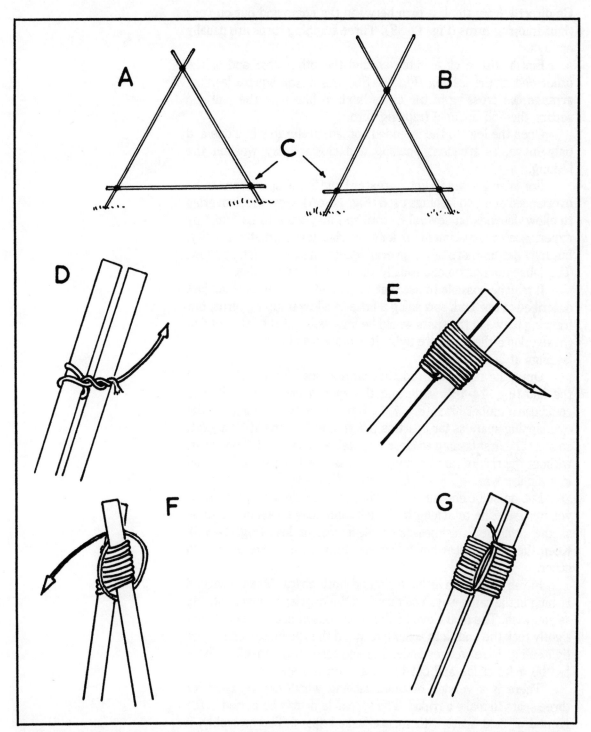

Fig. 14-3. *Sheer lashing* is used where spars have to be spread (A,B). Turns go around the spars (D,E), then spread and frapped (F,G).

Go directly from the last turn between the spars and put on very tight frapping turns (Fig. 14-3F). Three frapping turns are usually enough.

Finish with a clove hitch around the other spar and at the other end of the lashing (Fig. 14-3G). As in the square lashing, arrange the crossing of the clove hitch in line with the pull and secure the end under a frapping turn.

Open the legs to the intended spread, preferably in a one and only move, as frequent opening and closing may weaken the lashing.

For joining spars to get a greater length, the spars have to be overlapped and two lashings used (Fig. 14-4A). How much overlap to allow depends on several factors and may have to be found by experience or experiment. A long overlap gives greater rigidity, but may use up more of the overall length than you wish to allow. The joining arrangement usually must be a compromise.

It may be possible to use that version of the sheer lashing just described at one end, spreading a little to allow frapping turns, but frapping between the spars would be impossible at the other end of the overlap if the turns are tight. It is more usual to have the same lashings at both ends.

Draw the two spars together with a clove hitch and twist in the end (Fig. 14-4B). If getting the spars close is difficult, you could use a timber hitch (Fig. 7-4). Having the two lashings on the overlapping spars as far apart as possible makes the stiffest joint, so start the first lashing as close as possible to the end of one spar, without the risk of turns coming off, then treat the second lashing in a similar way.

Put on sufficient turns, drawing each as tight as possible as you make it. The total length of the lashing may be about the same as the combined thicknesses of the poles, or less (Fig. 14-4C). Keep the turns close, but be careful they do not ride over each other.

Finish with a clove hitch around both spars. Make a second lashing in the same way. You may find the overlap is now as strong as you wish. The final clove hitches may loosen in use if you do not tightly tuck the ends into lashing turns. If the lashings need further tightening, drive wedges under the end turns (Fig. 14-4D). These can be quite crude and cut by an axe on the spot.

There is a version of sheer lashing which can be used for three spars to make a tripod. The spread legs may be buried in the ground or held apart with square-lashed spars. The assembly, if

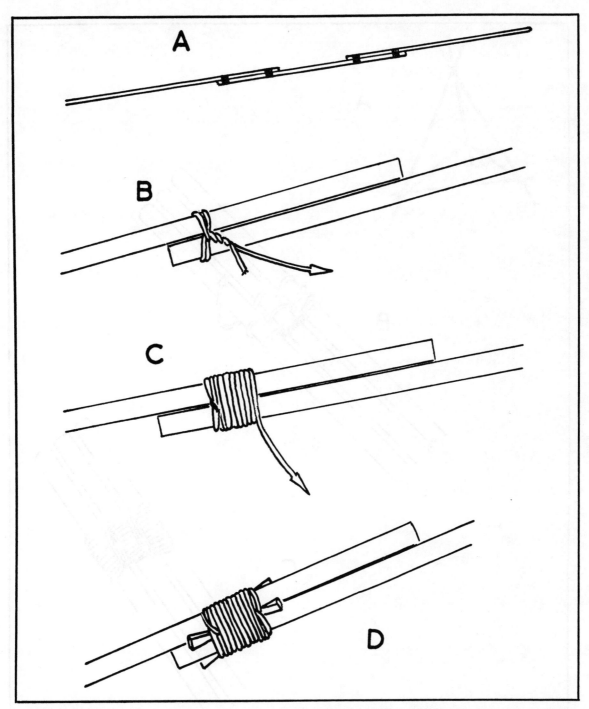

Fig. 14-4. Sheer lashing for lengthening poles is made without frapping turns (A,B,C), but can be tightened with wedges (D).

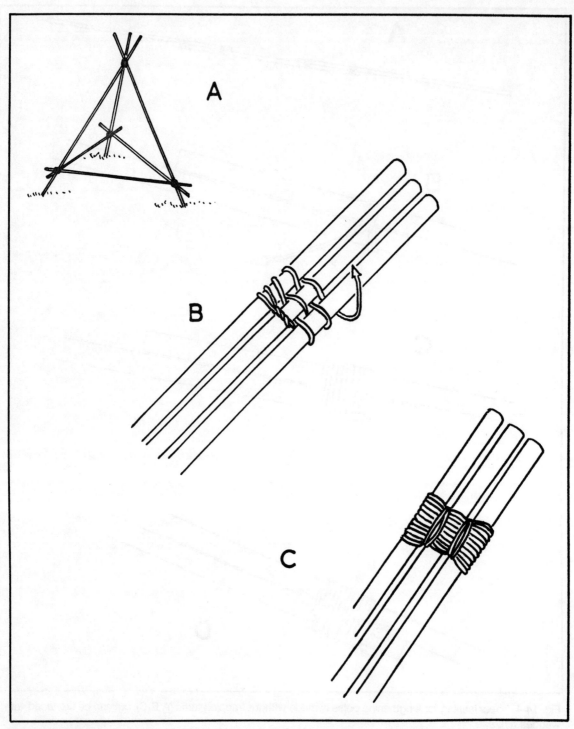

Fig. 14-5. If three poles are to form legs (A), the sheer lashing is taken in a figure eight fashion and frapped in both spaces (B,C).

used to support tackle for lifting a heavy weight, may then be called a *gyn* (Fig. 14-5A).

Some authorities suggest bringing the three spars together so the center one is opposite to the other two, but you then have to get the lashing tension just right if the legs are to spread correctly and the rope will be tight enough in the final position. It is easier to have all three spars the same way, with their tops level.

Start with a clove hitch on one outer spar and twist the end in. Take the line with an over and under action around the spars (Fig. 14-5B). The number of turns should not be very great. A total close-up length not much more than the diameter of one spar may be enough. The tension you apply depends mainly on the amount of final spread on the legs. You may have to make a trial spread before adjusting the rope.

Hold the tension on the rope while you, or an assistant, open the spars slightly. Add frapping turns (Fig. 14-5C). Three in each space should be satisfactory. Tighten them enough to compress the main turns as much as possible. Finish with a clove hitch on a different spar from where you started.

As with the two-legged arrangement, it is advisable to open to the final spread once only, so have your retaining spars and lashing ropes ready to complete the gyn. There will be two square lashings on each leg, but keep them close together.

Chapter 15

Decorative Knotting

There are a very large number of knots which are primarily decorative, and there is a tremendous amount of satisfaction to be gained from producing decorative rope or cord patterns. Some require much time and skill, as well as patience. This is not a book on ornamental knotting, but two examples are given of knotting, in which the result can be both useful and ornamental.

Although it is possible to form ornamental knots in any material from fine thread up to large ropes, there are some attractively-colored cords available, with braided construction, which display patterns better than undyed cord or those with three-stranded construction. The practical purpose may require the decorative piece of knotting to be in the more drab natural color, but where you want to give the best appearance to your work, colored cord is worthwhile. In some cases, you can use two colors together. These cords, in diameters up to a little over ⅛-inch, are sometimes sold by craft stores as *poly cords*—an abbreviation of the chemical name of the base material.

The word *sinnet* or *sennit* is the term for a long piece of knotting, which may also be known as a *plait*. Most people know how to plait three strands together, as in dealing with a girl's long hair. It is not much more difficult to do the same thing with four strands. Either plait will look attractive in two, three, or four different colored cords. There are many other plaits of this type with other numbers of parts, but a sinnet of different construction has been given a great variety of names, one of which is *Portugese sinnet.* Other knot tiers may know it as a *bosun's plait,* probably more correctly spelled *boatswain's plait.* In sailing ship days, it was popular for knife and pipe lanyards. It makes a good dog's lead, the three slings for a plant pot holder, or you can work it around a flexible electric cord.

The action of making the Portugese sinnet is forming a series of reef, or square knots, with granny knots to get a different effect. This is done around a core. For most purposes, the core may be two cords of similar diameter to the working cords, but the core may be a single thicker cord or even a rigid rod. If it is an electric cable you wish to cover, that forms the core.

The core should be the length you wish the sinnet to be. The working cords should be about three times this length, but this depends on tightness and closeness of working, and you may have to experiment with the amount you allow. The core could be one color and the working cords a different one.

For a practice length of Portugese sinnet, it is convenient to use one piece of cord doubled back twice (Fig. 15-1A). The center loop will be the core, and the long ends will be worked over it. Make an overhand knot at the top, to hang over a hook or nail (Fig. 15-1B). Working is easier if the core strands are stretched reasonably rigid, which you can achieve by attaching the bottom of the loop to your belt.

Put one working end across behind the core strands and in front of the other working strand (Fig. 15-1C). Lift the other strand over the front of the core strands and down through the loop of the first working strand (Fig. 15-1D) to make an overhand knot. Some workers prefer to cross in front and make the action the other way up. This does not matter, as the resulting sinnet will be the same. This basic action is all you have to master.

Do the same again from the other side. The result is a reef knot made round the core (Fig. 15-1E). Continue doing this in turn from alternate sides and the result will be a flat sinnet (Fig. 15-1F). Each time you twist the working strands together, pull them tightly outwards and upwards, so the knots fit close together for the neatest effect. Even if you want flexibility in the finished dog lead, or whatever you are making, close knotting will still be most satisfactory.

If you examine what you have done, you will see that you have reef knots across the core strands. If you make the action all from one side, instead of alternate sides, you will be forming granny knots. As a result, the sinnet will make itself into a twisted form without any encouragement from you (Fig. 15-1G). The

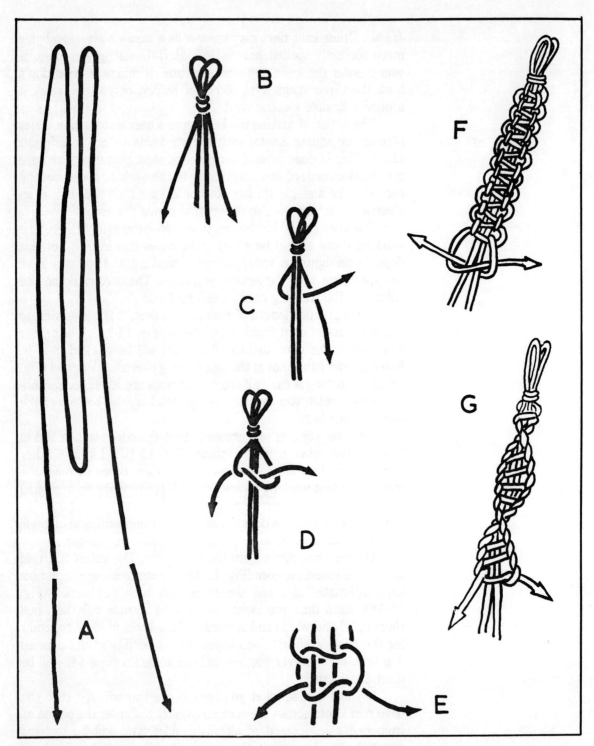

Fig. 15-1. *Portugese sinnet* can be made from a single cord (A–E) and may finish flat (F) or twisted (G).

twist can be either way, depending on the side on which you continue to work. On a long construction, you could alternate sections of flat sinnet with sections twisted in opposite ways.

If you want to make a long piece of Portugese sinnet, you have to deal with very long cords. For a dog lead 4 feet long, the working ends will start about 12 feet long, and that is a lot of cord to pull through every time, so any technique which reduces the tediousness is worth considering.

Most of the surplus line at each side may be wound on to small shuttles, which could be just temporary pieces up to 3 inches long cut from card (Fig. 15-2A). Put a rubber band over the wound cord, then draw out as you work your way down the sinnet. Another way to get the same effect without the shuttle is to form the cord into a "(butterfly.)" Twist the surplus cord in figure-eight manner around your thumb and little finger (Fig. 15-2B). Twist a rubber band tightly around the center (Fig. 15-2C), then you can draw out cord as needed without having to release the band.

For making a flat sinnet, but not the twisted version, there is a method of forming the square knot by only pulling through one working end, so cutting the possibly tedious tucking by half. Put a loop of working cord from one side over the core cords, with enough slack to allow finger and thumb to be put through (Fig. 15-2D). Reach through behind the core (Fig. 15-2E) and pull through two parts of the working cord (Fig. 15-2F), to extend far enough for the other working end to be passed down through (Fig. 15-2G). Notice that the end goes through the loops from opposite sides. Pull outwards in opposite directions, gripping above and below the knot (Fig. 15-2H), so the originally straight line is drawn across and the normal square knot results (Fig. 15-2J).

One of the best-known ornamental knots is the *Turk's head*. There is no satisfactory explanation of why Turkey comes into it, and the knot is not much like a head, but unlike so many other knots this is the universally accepted name, without the usual string of alternatives.

In its basic form (called four-bight three-lead to distinguish it from other versions), this is a continuous three-strand plait, which may be doubled or trebled (Fig. 15-3A). It may be tight round a pole or large rope, in which case it may act as a stopper or marker, as well as being decorative. If the cord is stiff, or the finished knot is stiffened with glue or varnish, the Turk's head could be a free ring, to hold a napkin or for some other purpose. A flattened version will make a mat or coaster.

There are an almost infinite variety of Turk's heads with

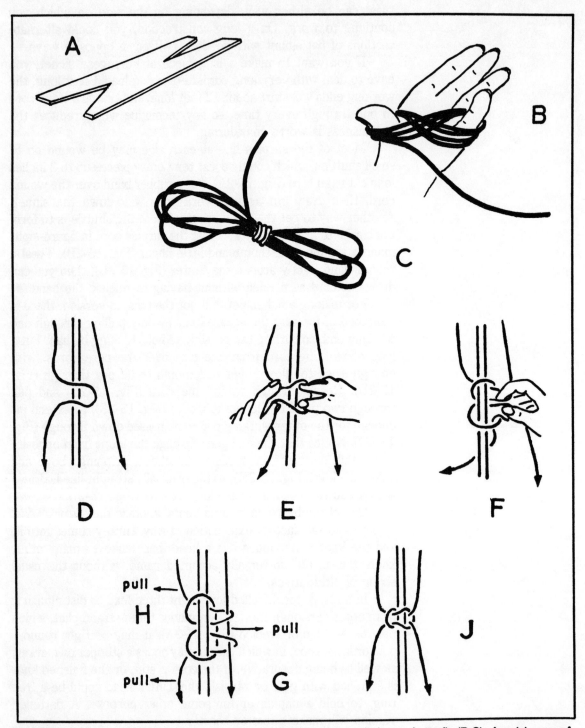

Fig. 15-2. Excess working cord may go on a *shuttle* (A) or be made into a *butterfly* (B,C). A quick way of forming a flat knot needs only one long end pulling through (D–J).

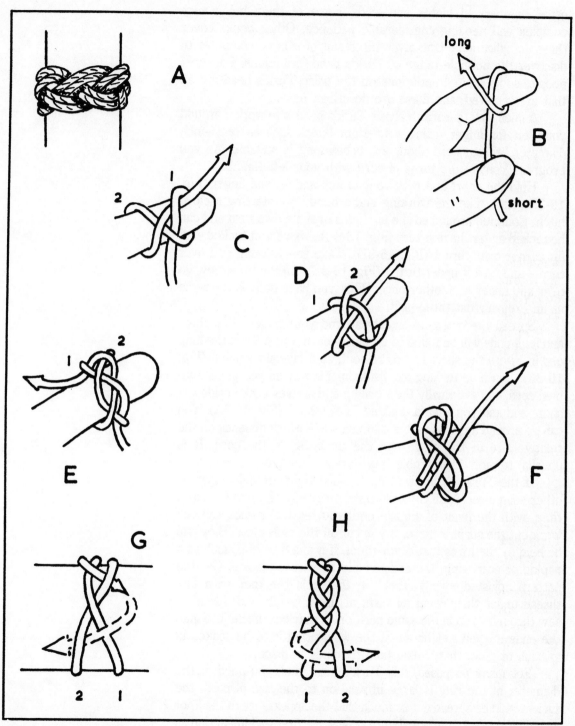

Fig. 15-3. A basic *Turk's head* (A) may be started around a finger (B–F) and the pattern extended, if required (G,H).

other numbers of bights and leads, some of them being very complex and needing considerable patience. Other books cover these complications. One gives the result of using a computer to discover the possible range of Turk's head formations. For most people, some limited variations on the basic Turk's head are all that are required, and these are described here.

A good way to learn the basic Turk's head is to work it around your left forefinger, using your right hand. A piece of ⅛-inch diameter braided cord about 24 inches long is suitable. As you progress, control the turns of cord with your left thumb.

Hold the short end with your thumb and second finger (Fig. 15-3B), then take the working end around as if starting a clove hitch. Continue around so the end goes over its own turn and can be tucked under the first turn (Fig. 15-3C). Above that tucked end, lift turn 2 over turn 1 (Fig. 15-3D). Take the working end over turn 2 and tuck it under turn 1 (Fig. 15-3E). All the turns now go over and under each other once. What you have done is the same as an ordinary flat three-plait.

Spread the crossings evenly around your finger. The short and long ends will be found to be facing each other. Tuck the long end in where the short end comes out, so it lays alongside it (Fig. 15-3F). Continue tucking alongside in this way so you get a doubled cord, and eventually the working end arrives back beside the short end and you have a doubled Turk's head (Fig. 15-3A). You can go around again to treble it, if you wish. Much depends on the relative size of the circle and the thickness of the cord. It is unusual to more than treble this Turk's head knot.

If the Turk's head is to be finished tight around a spar or other solid object, pull the cord tight progressively, one tuck at a time, with the point of a spike until you reach the ends and can work out the surplus there. If you cut off the ends close, they will be held by the turns that cover them. If it is a free ring, such as a napkin or scarf ring, the ends should be secured inside. Get the pattern adjusted evenly, then tie the ends together with fine thread under their covering turn, or use a needle and thread to sew through them in the same position. It may be sufficient to glue the ends to their neighbors. If the whole ring is to be soaked in varnish or glue, that should hold the ends in place.

For many purposes, this Turk's head is all you need. If the diameter of the ring is large in relation to the size of cord, the tucks would be spread out so much that the appearance of the knot would be spoiled. It is possible to repeat the first tucking action as often as necessary to fill up a large ring. You can make such a

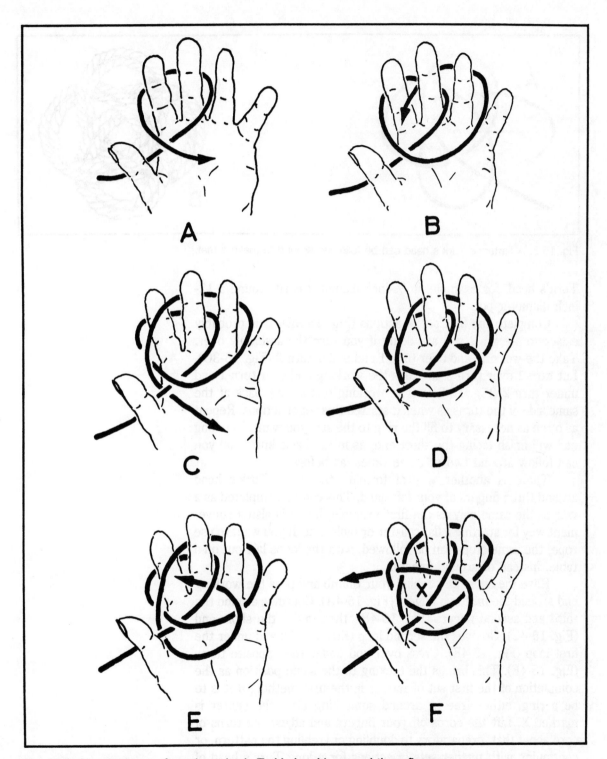

Fig. 15-4. A second way of starting a basic Turk's head is around three fingers.

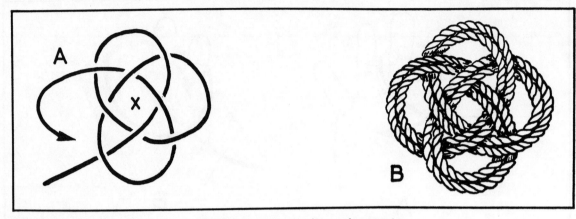

Fig. 15-5. A flattened Turk's head can be followed around to make a mat.

Turk's head, for example, in ⅛-inch diameter cord around a 12-inch diameter pot.

Complete the first set of actions (Fig. 15-3E). It is probably easier to see what you are doing if you turn the assembly over. Take the working end over turn 1 and under turn 2 (Fig. 15-3G). Lift turn 1 over turn 2 and tuck the working end over turn 1 and under turn 2 (Fig. 15-3H). The working end is now back at the same side of the turns as when it started this set of actions. Repeat as often as necessary to fill the ring to the size you want. The long end will finish facing the short end, as in the basic knot, and you can follow around two or three times, as before.

There is another way of forming the same Turk's head around three fingers of your left hand. This can be completed as a ring in the same way as the first example, but it is also a convenient way for starting a flat coaster or table mat. If you want to use rope, the same steps can be followed, with the loops laid out on a table, instead of around fingers.

Have the short end behind your thumb and pass the working end around the first two fingers (Fig. 15-4A). Continue around the third and second fingers (Fig. 15-4B), then under the short end (Fig. 15-4C). Go over the second loop (Fig. 15-4D) and under the first loop (Fig. 15-4E). Cross over and under the opposite turns (Fig. 15-4F). This brings the tucking to the same position as the completion of the first set of actions in the first method. If it is to be a ring, either free or around something else, the center is marked X. Lift the cords off your fingers and adjust the turns of cord about that, preparatory to doubling or trebling the pattern, or continuing with further sets of actions for a long Turk's head of larger diameter.

For a flat mat, lift the cord off your fingers and put it, as it is, flat on a table. Adjust it so all spaces, including the center are about the same size. Take the working end in alongside the short end, so it forms the final loop (Fig. 15-5A). Continue around to double or treble the pattern (Fig. 15-5B). Arrange the ends under crossing turns and secure them by sewing or tying with thread. In its doubled form, this is the badge of the *International Guild of Knot Tyers.*

Chapter 16

Splicing

Splicing differs from other forms of knotting in that it uses separate strands instead of the whole thickness of the rope. Joints are mostly made by intertwining strands instead of twisting ropes or cords together. Splicing is commonly done with three-strand rope, but there are ways of splicing the various forms of braided rope. Some of the new types of braided rope, with cores which are either braided or three-strand, involve special splices to suit the particular construction, and many rope manufacturers provide instructions for their own ropes.

It is the common form of right-hand-laid three-strand rope which most users need to splice. Although there are splices for joining and other purposes, by far the most commonly needed splice is an *eye splice* for putting a loop in the end of a rope. It is usual to treat a slice as permanent. Although it is not impossible to take apart a splice, the lay of the rope is disturbed, and it is not left in such a normal form as if a knot was used and untied. If you need a temporary loop, use a bowline or one of the other knots, but an eye splice is both stronger and neater if the loop is intended to be permanent.

A properly made splice should never come apart under load. It may not be quite as strong as the rope, but it is nearer to it than any knot and, in practice, the rope would break before any part of the splice severs. In an eye splice (and with many other splices), the individual strands tuck over and under each other so the effect of a load is to squeeze them tighter together.

Ropes are laid up in varying degrees of tightness to suit their intended uses. This affects the ease of splicing, which is also affected by the material from which the rope is made. Most natural fiber ropes are more amenable to tucking. Some synthetic ropes are difficult to open and tuck, but three-strand rope in any material can be spliced in the same way; although some may require more care and patience.

An eye splice is made in the same way, whatever the form of loop. It may be an eye for hooking over a post, it could be a large loop to sit in, it might be tight around a rod, or it could be fitted to a metal thimble. The important part is the tucked length (Fig. 16-1A). Although three-strand material of any size from cord up to the largest rope can be spliced, for practice it is advisable to use rope about ½-inch thick, not too tightly laid and of not too stiff a material. You can then see what is happening, and the strands are fairly easy to manipulate.

With most natural fiber ropes, you do not have a problem of unintentional unlaying, but with synthetic rope you must take precautions to keep both rope and strands as you want them. For a first attempt, this may be advisable with natural fiber rope. With rope about ½-inch diameter, unlay at least 6 inches and either bind with electrician's tape or put on a temporary seizing (Fig. 16-1B), which may be a few turns of knotted thread or a constrictor knot. Seal the ends of the opened strands or temporarily whip them.

You will have to open the strands in the main part of the rope to tuck the end strands. Try the tightness of the lay by holding a section of rope and twisting in opposite directions (Fig. 16-1C). If you are unable to open the lay enough to pass an end strand, you will need a spike to force a wider gap. There are some spikes with grooved sides, so that you can leave the spike in place and slide the end strand along it, but with a plain spike you force the opening and put in the end strand as soon as you withdraw the spike, before the gap has closed.

Put the end strands across the main part of the rope at the point where you want to make the splice, with two end strands in front across the lay of the rope (Fig. 16-1D). Lift a main strand and push end #2 under it (Fig. 16-1E).

Lift the next main strand on the loop side of #2 end so you can tuck end #1 under it, going in the space where end #2 comes out (Fig. 16-1F). You now have two strands under two main strands, so there must be a main strand with nothing under it. Find this and tuck end #3 under it, in the same direction as the other two (Fig. 16-1G).

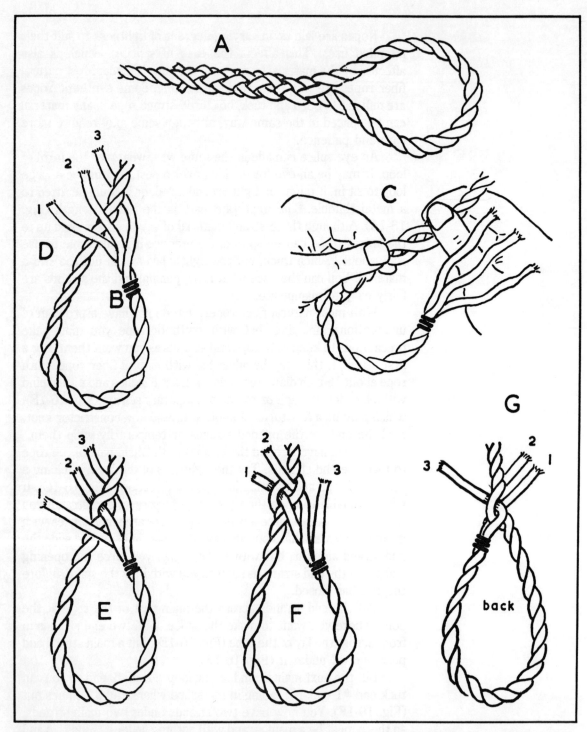

Fig. 16-1. In an eye splice, the strands are tucked into the standing part several times (A). The splice is started by tucking the end strands under three main strands (B–G).

Pull the three ends tight and get them into the same level around the rope. Common faults at this stage are uneven tension and ends projecting at different levels. If you have worked correctly, you will have tucked so one end projects from each space (Fig. 16-2A).

The next step is to make another round of tucks. Take any end strand and tuck it over the main strand next to it and into the next space—over and under one (Fig. 16-2B). Do this with the second and third end strands. Pull the ends tight and coax them into the same plane and fairly close to the first round of tucks. A common fault is to go too far up the rope and leave the tucks there. The tucked ends should go around the rope at about the same angle as the main strands, but in the opposite direction.

Make a third round of tucks in the same way, pulling each end tight in turn. In hairy natural fiber rope, a total of three tucks may be enough, but in smooth synthetic rope, it is usual to tuck four or five times (Fig. 16-1A). These are called *full tucks,* and they may be followed by various finishing arrangements.

For some purposes, it is sufficient to cut off the ends a short distance outside the last tucks and seal synthetic fibers. Be careful not to melt any part of the splice with a flame. A seizing could be put over the cut ends for a neat finish. A sufficient length of turns made like a West Country whipping will do. The tucked part of the rope will be twice the circumference of the untucked rope. To avoid an abrupt change of section there should be a round of *taper tucks.* After the full tucks, use a knife to scrape each strand to about half thickness, then tuck these tapered parts before cutting off. If appearance and smoothness of finish are not so important, the strongest finish for a splice is *dog-knotting.* After the final full tucks, divide the fibers of each strand into two, then seize adjoining groups together (Fig. 16-2C), before cutting off. Remove any temporary seizings. On board a sailing ship, the splice was finished by rolling the tucked part underfoot, but ashore, grit will be avoided if this is done between two boards.

If the splice has to fit around something solid, it is made in the same way, but you have to position the tucks so the finished splice is not slack, yet not so tight that there are open parts of end strands outside the splice. A common arrangement is around a thimble (Fig. 16-2D), which protects the rope from wear if it is on a metal fitting.

Prepare the splicing in the normal way. Tuck end #2 where you think it should be. Close up on the thimble. If necessary, slide the tucked end up or down to get the fit you want. Loosen the tuck

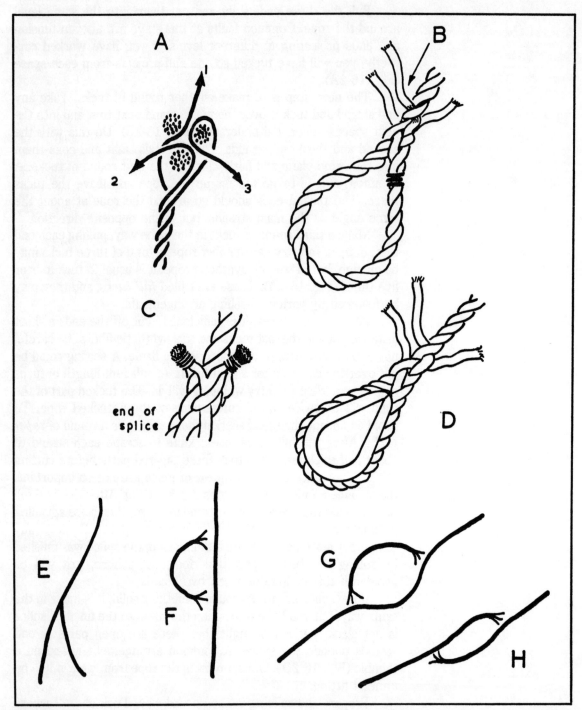

Fig. 16-2. After the first tucks, one end projects from each space. (A) Another round of tucks is started (B). Ends could be dog-knotted (C). A thimble may be included (D) or the method used for other constructions (E–H).

and take out the thimble. Tuck the other two ends loosely. Put the thimble in and draw the ends tight. If the fit is satisfactory, remove the temporary seizing and tighten finally on the thimble. Continue other tucks in the same way as before.

The technique of eye splicing can be used for other situations. One rope may be spliced into the side of another rope. If you want two tails to a single rope, one rope to make the fork can be spliced into the other in exactly the same way as for an eye splice (Fig. 16-2E). If you want a loop on the side of a rope, a suitable piece can be tucked in the same way (Fig. 16-2F). If you want a loop in line with the rope, the same method can be used, allowing the main rope and the addition to be the same length (Fig. 16-2G). Another way of getting this result is to overlap the ends of two ropes and splice them into each other (Fig. 16-2H). This would also be a way of joining ropes, which may then be twisted around each other between the tucked parts.

Chapter 17

Netmaking Knots

If a piece of netting is examined, the knots between the meshes will be seen to be sheet bends, except in a small amount of decorative netting. This applies whether the net is made with small meshes and fine line or with heavy rope and large meshes. Netmaking, or *braiding*, involves tying very large numbers of sheet bends, even in a net of modest size. There are special techniques to speed the work and ensure accuracy, instead of the tedious action of tying individual knots in the usual way.

It is possible to do a small amount of netmaking without special tools. The few meshes needed to repair a damaged net can be gauged for size with the fingers. For regular netmaking the mesh size is controlled by a *mesh stick* or gauge (Fig. 17-1A), which is a piece of thin wood slightly narrower than the "bar" of a mesh (Fig. 17-1B). Round the edges and corners. You need a separate mesh stick for each size mesh. Some workers favor a short stick, but a longer one is easy to handle.

You will be using a considerable length of line, which has to be gathered up to avoid having to pull through a long piece. It is possible to make the line into a butterfly (Fig. 15-2), but it is more usual to use a needle or shuttle, which can be made or bought. The needle must be small enough to pass easily through a mesh, but you can get more on a large needle, when the mesh is large enough to pass it, so if much netting is to be made, several sizes of needles may be advisable.

One type of needle has slightly open jaws (Fig. 17-1C). An-

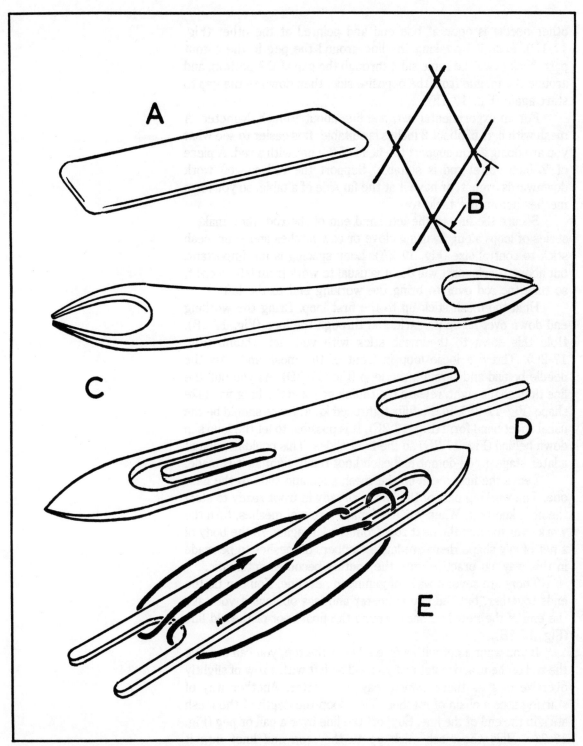

Fig. 17-1. A *mesh stick* (A) sets the size of the net mesh (B). Line is wound on a needle (C,D,E).

other needle is open at one end and pointed at the other (Fig. 17-1D). Load it by taking the line around the peg in the cutout part, back down the same side, through the gap at the bottom, and around the tongue from the opposite side, then down to the gap to start again (Fig. 17-1E).

For an experimental net, use line about ⅛-inch diameter. A mesh with bars of about 2 inches is suitable. It is easier to see what you are doing if you support the head of the net with a rod. A piece of ½-inch dowel rod is suitable. Support the rod so you work downwards from it, or have it at the far side of a table, so you form meshes across the table top.

Secure the line to the left-hand end of the rod, then make a series of loops along it, using clove or cow hitches and your mesh stick to control size (Fig. 17-2A). Loop spacing is not important, but about 1-inch apart will do. It is usual to work from left to right, so turn the rod over to bring the working end to the left.

Hold the mesh stick up to the first loop. Bring the working end down over it, up its back, and through the loop (Fig. 17-2B). Hold this down to the mesh stick with your left thumb (Fig. 17-2C). Throw a loose loop in front of the mesh and pass the needle behind and through the loop (Fig. 17-2D). As you pull the line tight to the right, release the thumb grip and the knot will take shape (Fig. 17-2E). In the fully tightened knot, there should be the usual sheet bend form (Fig. 17-2F). It is possible to let the loop slip down behind (Fig. 17-2G) so the knot slides. This could happen at a later stage if you do not pull each knot really tight as it is made.

Leave the first mesh on the mesh stick and slide to the next one. The working part of the line is already in front ready to start the next knotting. When you have made a row of meshes, turn the work over to start the next row from the left again. In the body of a net of any shape there are large numbers of meshes to be made in this way, so practice until the routine becomes automatic.

There are several ways of joining in new line. You can tie the ends together, but the join is neater and less obvious if you take the end of the new line back around the final knot of the old line (Fig. 17-2H).

If you want a net with a free edge at the top, you can remove the rod of the practice net and you will be left with a row of slightly oversize meshes there, which may not matter. Another way of starting uses a chain of meshes. Tie a loop the depth of the mesh stick in the end of the line. Support the line over a nail or peg (Fig. 17-3A). Hold the mesh stick up to the loop and knot into it (Fig. 17-3B). Drop to the bottom of that mesh and do it again (Fig.

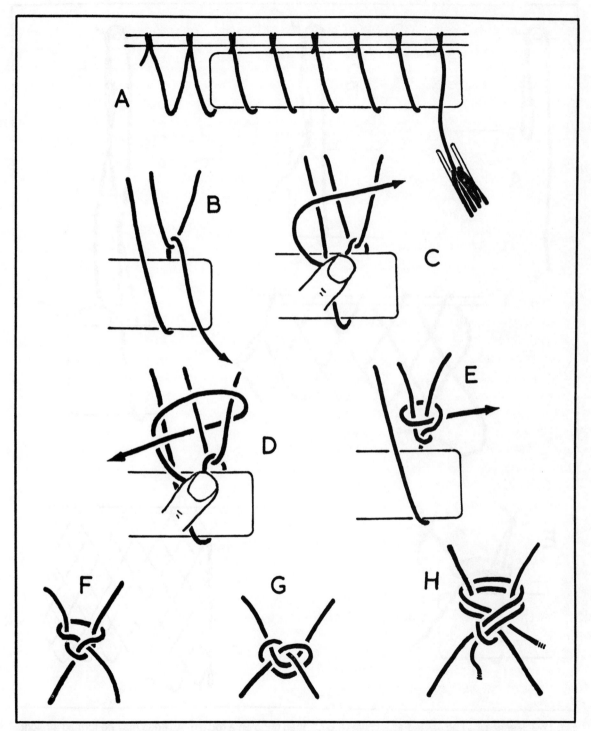

Fig. 17-2. A net may be started on a rod (A). Knotting is done over the mesh stick (B–E). The finished knot (F) should not be allowed to fall out of shape (G). New line follows round the knot (Fig. 17-2H).

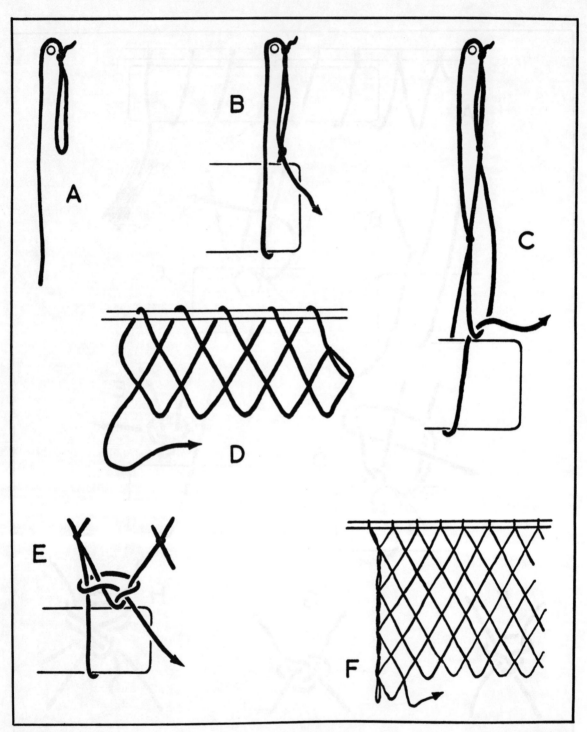

Fig. 17-3. Meshes may be started as a chain (A,B,C), then hung on a rod (D). An edge may be formed straight (E,F).

17-3C). Continue in this way until you have made enough meshes. Allow for the fact that you are forming two rows in this chain.

It would be possible to add on more meshes with all the first meshes hung on one peg, but it is easier to see what you are doing if you support the net on a rod (Fig. 17-3D). When you have made several more rows of meshes, the early parts may be transferred to the peg. At any stage of any net, it is always helpful to have something to pull against, so a rod, nail, or peg higher up the net is advisable.

Unless you do something about it, a net will have diamond meshes on all four edges. In some constructions, you may want this, so a supporting line can be passed through. If it would be better to have straight edges, this is easy to arrange after the first row. Work across in the usual way, but at the side, take in the side of the mesh being formed as well as the one above it (Fig. 17-3E). This gives you a straight hanging loop to join into when you make the next row. The doubled edge (Fig. 17-3F) also provides strength.

The nets described so far have diamond meshes. You can pull the net longer and reduce its width at the same time. Its external sizes can be altered quite a lot. That may be what you want, but for some purposes the net has to keep its shape. An example is a tennis net. Instead of the meshes being diagonal to the edges (Fig. 17-4A), they have to be parallel (Fig. 17-4B). Such a net uses normal knots in the body of the net, but they must be of increasing and decreasing sizes at the edges.

Treat a square-mesh net as a diamond-mesh one with its top at one corner. Make two meshes as if starting a chain (Fig. 17-4C). Make a second mesh in the side of the first (Fig. 17-4D). You can continue to add meshes while the chain is hanging, but it is easier to see what is happening in the drawings if the meshes are opened out.

Go down the side of the third mesh and make an overhand knot to it (Fig. 17-4E) diagonally in line with the other knots. Work back across the two main meshes and make a third new mesh by knotting into the side of the end one above and down to knot into its own side (Fig. 17-4F). Continue making rows of meshes in this way, bringing the line down the sides of meshes at alternate ends, building the pattern until the bottom corner has been reached. To turn the corner, omit the final mesh in the following row (Fig. 17-4G). As you return to the bottom edge with each row of meshes, reduce by tying into the side of the previous mesh each time.

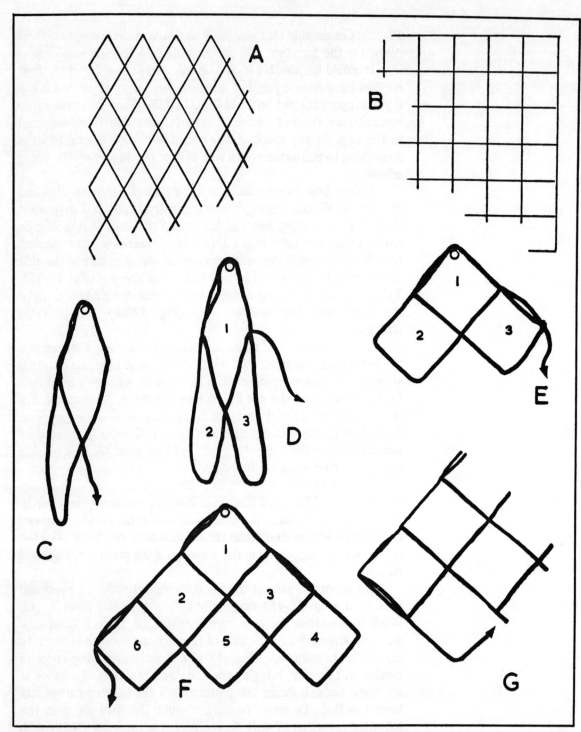

Fig. 17-4. Diamond (A) and square (B) meshes can be made. A square mesh net is worked from a corner (C–G).

The other edge goes on increasing until you have made sufficient length, then the rows are reduced at both ends until only one mesh is left at the bottom right corner.

For a square-mesh net to finish a good shape and be symmetrical, all meshes must be made carefully to size. In a diamond-mesh net, individual mesh sizes are not so critical, so if that type is acceptable for your purpose, it is preferable.

If a hole in a net has to be repaired, you will probably have to cut away further so the new line can follow a regular path. Examine an existing knot to see which way up the net was made. Work the repair the same way, if possible. Arrange to start at a "three-legged" mesh (one with three out of four of the bars still projecting from the old knot). Knot your new line over that knot and work across the bottoms of the old meshes. Trim old meshes at the end so you can knot in and work back across with a new row. When you are near the end of filling the gap, trim if necessary, so you finish on another three-legged mesh.

Chapter 18

Macramé Knots

Macramé is a name believed to have come from an Arabic word which originally meant fringe, but it is now applied to one art of creative knotting in which a large range of objects, such as bags, wall decorations, holders, and hangers of many types, are made by building up patterns with knots. The often seemingly complicated articles are made with large numbers of simple knots.

Macramé has been practiced in natural fiber cords for many centuries, but it is the coming of attractive synthetic cords which has caused a revival of interest. These cords allow articles to be made in many colors, and their nature allows other decorations that are impossible with most natural cords. Synthetics also have the advantage of resistance to rot, so such things as pot hangers can be used outside or in other damp conditions.

This is obviously not a book of macramé designs, but the reader who is attracted to the way simple knots can be built up into interesting patterns can find details of things to make in the many macramé pattern books available.

Macramé workers tend to have their own names for some knots, different from the names other knot tiers use, but it will be seen that all of them are the same as knots already described for other circumstances, although some may be combined in different ways. For nearly all macramé construction, the knots are based on the half hitch and the overhand knot, which may be called a *half knot*.

The half hitch may be needed around a rod or another cord.

Two will make a clove hitch, more likely to be called a *double half hitch* in instructions (Fig. 18-1A). This could be made triple or more. Many designs start on a holding cord, pinned to the working board (Fig. 18-1B). The working cords are usually attached to it with lark's head knots (Fig. 18-1C and D). There could be a half hitch each side of the lark's head knot. If this is carried further, it is a *tatted bar knot* (Fig. 18-1E). For handles and similar things, any of these knots may be on rods or metal rings.

Much macramé work is based on what will be seen to be the same as Portugese sinnet or bosun's plait (Fig. 15-1), although the pattern may be over a large area instead of a single row. A macramé worker calls the basic form a *half knot* and the second step makes it a *square knot* (Fig. 18-2A). In some patterns, it is necessary to make the design symmetrical by tying the knots on one side the opposite way to the other, so you have to learn a *right-hand square knot* (Fig. 18-2B) and a *left-hand square knot* (Fig. 18-2C). Facility in making these knots either way will come with practice. This is important, as large numbers of square knots have to be made in many projects.

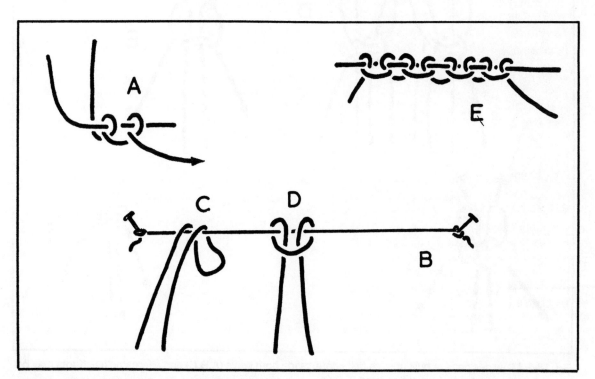

Fig. 18-1. Basic macramé knots include half hitches and *lark's head knots* over a holding cord.

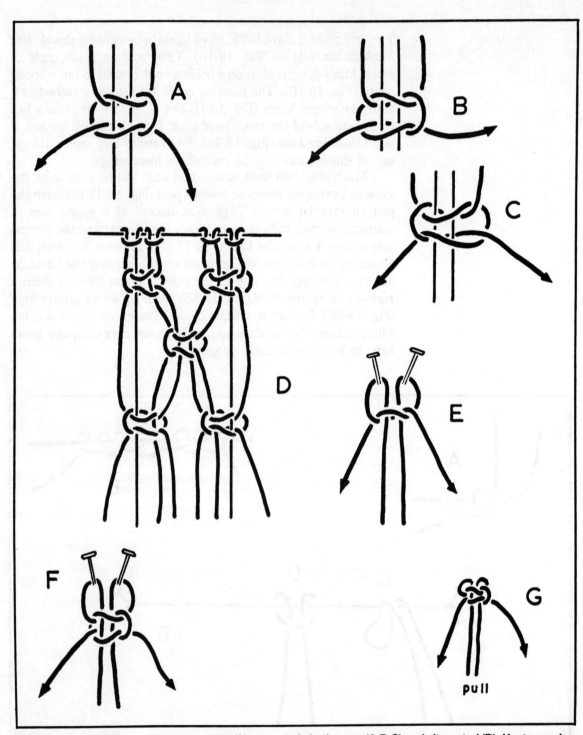

Fig. 18-2. Many designs are built up with half knots, made both ways (A,B,C) and alternated (D). Knots may be started on pins instead of a holding cord (E,F,G).

An area of knotting, as required in anything flat and usually densely packed (such as the side of a bag) is made by making *alternating square knots*. In this, what were the working cords in one horizontal row of knots become the filler cords or core in the next row, and the previous filler cords are worked around them. For simplicity, only two starting square knots are shown (Fig. 18-2D), but the method is the same whatever width is built up. Put the cords on the holding cord in groups of four.

As drawn, construction is shown open, but in most work, the knots are made close up, so a finished panel of any width and depth has only small gaps, and the effect is a tight mass of knots. At an edge, the outer working and filler cords continue down, but across the width of the construction, the working and filler cords alternate as you progress down the panel.

Not all projects are suitable for starting on a holding cord. Many start on pins. Only two are shown (Fig. 18-2E), but you can use whatever number are needed to make up the width required. Form a row of square knots (Fig. 18-2F). Remove the pins and pull down the filler cords to tighten on each knot (Fig. 18-2G). Join as many of these formations as are necessary to make the width with alternating square knots, so you can continue down in the same way as below a holding cord.

An edge may be tapered by leaving out end knots in each or alternate rows. The resulting free cords may be used in joining opposite panels of a bag or similar assembly. In some projects, the cords have to be brought together at the end of a panel so they hang down centrally. This is arranged with half hitches inwards from each side, in what is called an *accumulating edge knot*. Normally, there are alternating square knots immediately above, but to avoid confusion, the drawing (Fig. 18-3) shows them coming straight down. In the example, there are twelve cords. The two central ones hang straight down, and the others are brought in to them. Only work on the left side is shown. The right side has to be made symmetrical to it.

Bring in the outer cord and make two half hitches with the next cord over it tightly (Fig. 18-3A). Put the cord that has just formed the half hitches alongside the first. Make two half hitches over these two with the next cord (Fig. 18-3B). Again, pull tight. You now have three together. Use the next cord to make two half hitches round them (Fig. 18-3C). Do this once more around four cords (Fig. 18-3D). When you have done this at the other side as well, you finish with twelve cords close together (Fig. 18-3E), ready to make a tassel or be treated in some other way.

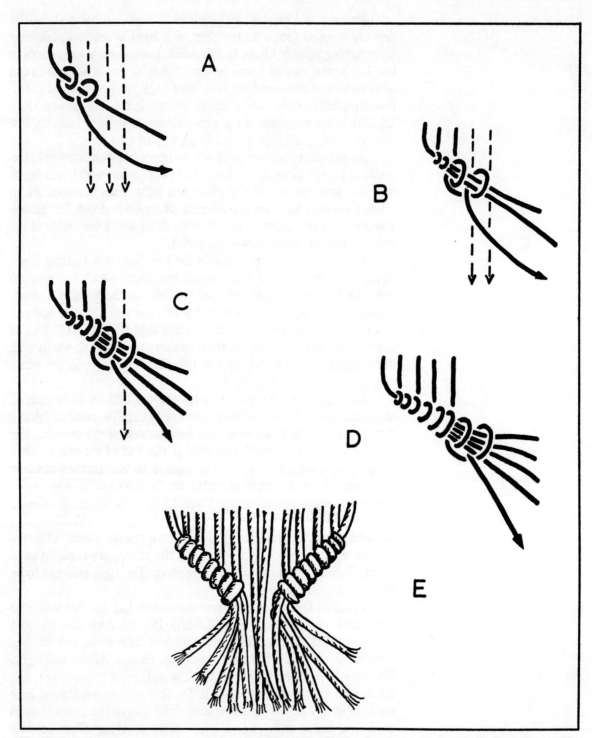

Fig. 18-3. Half hitches are used to build up accumulating edge knots when ends have to be brought to the center.

When a number of cords have to be bound tightly together, such as would be produced by using accumulating edge knots, a cord is used as a whipping or seizing, but a macramé worker calls this a *wrap knot*. Another different name is a *coil knot*, which is the same as a *blood knot* (Fig. 2-1F). A macramé *Josephine knot* is the equivalent of a *carrick bend* (Fig. 3-5), but it is used for decoration rather than joining.

Glossary

Glossary

There are a very large number of nautical knotting terms which date from the days of sailing ships. Only those which are likely to be met in everyday use are included amongst the more generally used terms.

adrift—A rope is adrift it comes out of place. A knot is adrift if it spills out of shape or comes undone.

alternate—In macramé: take half the cords from one knot and half the cords from an adjoining knot to form a new knot below them. The next row reverts to the first arrangement.

backhanded rope—Strands with a left-handed twist.

becket—A rope loop used as a handle or for attaching a hook.

bend—The knot used to tie two ropes together. The action of making such a knot.

bight—A loop in a rope, as when it is turned back on itself.

bitter end—The end of a rope opposite to the end that is being used for work.

bollard—A strong mooring point for a boat.

bowline—Originally one of the ropes used to trim a square sail, but now the name of the loop knot that was used at its end.

bowse—To haul a rope tight.

braid—To make netting or interweave strands to make a pattern.

braided rope or cord—Made with the outside yarns woven into each other diagonally around the circumference.

bridle—A span of rope which has its ends secured.

butterfly—Long line coiled and held with a band.

cable—A large rope made by twisting three smaller ropes together.

capsize—In knotting, to pull a knot out of shape so it slips.

carry away—Break or become undone.

cast off—Untie or cut so the rope becomes free.

clinch—Rope turned into a small eye and the overlaps seized together.

coir—Fibers from the outer husks of the coconut used to make rope that will float.

cording—In macramé: building up a pattern with half hitches.

core—A heart, in a multistrand rope, or the part around which other cords are worked in making some sinnets.

cow's tail—Unlaid or frayed end of rope

end for end—Turning a rope around to equalize wear in it.

eye—A loop or bight of rope with the ends crossing. A spliced loop.

fiber—The smallest element in the construction of a rope. It is more correct to use the term for natural materials and call the equivalent parts of synthetic rope *filaments*.

fid—Tapered wooden spike used for opening rope strands.

filament—The smallest element of man-made material that forms the fibers of synthetic rope.

frap—Put on turns around others to tighten them.

grommet—Endless circle of rope or cord. If long, it is a strop.

guy—A rope for steadying.

halliard or halyard—Rope for hoisting flags, sails, and similar things.

hard laid—Tightly twisted rope.

heart—A core strand or filler.

hemp—Fibers of the hemp plant, once one of the most popular fibers for rope before the introduction of synthetic materials.

hitch—A knot for joining a rope to something solid or to a much thicker rope

holding cord—In macramé: A stretched line on which other cords are knotted.

Irish pennant—Frayed end of rope.

jute—Coarse natural fiber used for making cordage.

knot—Now the general name for all fastenings with rope, but traditionally it was only formed in a single rope.

lanyard—Small rope for securing knives and similar things.

lash—Secure by binding with rope.

lay—The direction of twist in rope.

left-hand lay—Rope in which the strands twist away from you to the left as you look along it.

line—Common name for all kinds of cordage, often in preference to calling it rope.

long-jawed—Stretched rope that has lost much of its twist.

macramé—From Arabic *migramah,* meaning ornamental fringe or braid.

make fast—Secure a rope, usually by knotting.

manila—The name given to rope made from *abaca fiber,* obtained mainly from Manila. One of the finest rope materials before the coming of synthetic fibers.

marline spike—A metal spike used for opening rope strands.

mesh stick—Gauge for regulating the size of mesh in a net.

nylon—Synthetic material used for making cordage.

painter—Rope attached to the bow of a boat for mooring or towing it.

pay out—Allow to run out under control.

pricker—A spike with a handle.

purchase—A mechanical advantage, as when using tackle.

rack—Seize ropes together.

render—Ease off or slacken.

rope—Traditionally any cordage over ⅜-inch (10 mm) diameter, but the term is loosely applied.

right-hand lay—Rope in which the strands twist away from you to the right as you look along it.

round turn—Line completely encircling an object.

seizing—A lashing of small line around ropes.

set up—Tighten, as when tensioning guy lines.

sinnet or sennit—Interwoven lines in the form of a plait.

sheave—A pulley wheel over which a rope is put.

sisal—Fibers of the *henequin* plant used for a cheap and coarse type of natural fiber rope.

snub—Check the movement of a line by passing a turn around a post or something similar.

soft laid—Rope with loosely twisted strands.

splice—Join the end of a rope to its own standing part or to another rope by interweaving strands.

square knotting—Alternative name for macramé.

standing part—The main part of a rope away from its ends.

stick—Tuck, as when entering strands in a splice.

stop—Seize or lash, usually temporarily.

strand—The part of a rope made up of yarns twisted one way, then the strands are twisted the other way to make the rope.

strop or strap—A large endless rope. A small endless rope is a grommet.

swig—Pull out on the center of an already taut rope to gain a little more tension, which is taken up on a cleat or other attachment.

tackle—An arrangement of pulley blocks or rope loops to provide a purchase or mechanical advantage. Pronounced *'tayckle.'*

take a turn—Put a turn of rope on a cleat or other fitting.

thimble—Round or heart-shaped metal or plastic fitting, grooved for a rope spliced around it. It protects the eye of rope when attached to a metal fitting.

toggle—Small pin, usually wood, with a groove around its center, where a rope is spliced. This provides a fastening by linking with an open eye in another rope or its own other end. May also be any piece of wood put through a knot to allow quick release.

unbend—Untie, cast off, let loose.

unlay—Open rope to separate the strands.

veer—Allow a rope to run out gradually.

warp—A very large rope. The action of using such a rope to move a ship.

whip—Bind the end of a rope to prevent it unlaying.

whipcord—A tightly laid fine hemp cord. Besides its use in whips, it was much used for early macramé belts and similar items.

with the lay—Coiling rope in the direction it is laid, usually right-handed (clockwise).

yarn—Fibers twisted together as the first step in forming a rope.

Index

Index

Other Bestsellers From TAB

Other Bestsellers From TAB